Rainbows and Rhymes

This book is dedicated to the memory of
John Palmer RIP
8th February 1973 to 8th December 2010

Through sheer selfless determination, dedication
and the love for all of his family,
John ensured their hopes and dreams
came to fruition
by devoting endless time and sharing
precious moments
in producing and publishing a compilation of these
words of art in this wonderful book of
Rainbows and Rhymes.
By
Rene McDermott

Pax

Rainbows and Rhymes

Rene Mcdermott

Copyright © 2010 by Rene Mcdermott.

ISBN: Softcover   978-1-4535-8634-1
             Ebook   978-1-4535-8635-8

All rights reserved. No part of this book may be reproduced or transmitted in any form or by any means, electronic or mechanical, including photocopying, recording, or by any information storage and retrieval system, without permission in writing from the copyright owner.

This book was printed in the United States of America.

To order additional copies of this book, contact:
Xlibris Corporation
0-800-644-6988
www.xlibrispublishing.co.uk
Orders@xlibrispublishing.co.uk
300930

Introduction..11

ANIMALS

A Mouse Tale 15
Animal Crackers..16
Big Bad Wolf...17
Birds..18
Dancing Bear 19
Death of a Horse 20
Goldfish 21
Homeless...22
Leader of the Pack 23
Scruffy 24
Seals 25
The Badger Baiters 26
The Day of the Animals 27
The Foxes Lament 28
The Lost Chance 29
Vannie Gogh 31
White Lies...32

HUMOUR

Annabelle Jane...35
Bags 37
Be Mine 38
Cack-Handed Kate...39
Cheer Up 40
Diamonds are Forever 41
Feed Me 42

Gooday	43
I Want	44
Just A Girl	45
Marie	46
Naughty	47
Never Judge a Book by It's Cover	48
Nit Wit	50
No Will Power	51
Poor Little Rich Girl	52
Scandals	53
Sharing	54
Speed Freak	55
Temptation	56
The Diet	57
The Flight	58
The Frogs Lament	59
The Old Days	60
The Place to Be	61
The Star	63
The Sun Dodger	64
The Worried Egg	65
Traffic Wardens	66
What Matters Most	67
White and Wong	68
Why Do Things Always Go Wrong	69

FROM THE HEART

A Day in the Life of Misfortune	73
Always	74
Alzheimers	75
Balance of Poverty	76
Beyond the Vine	77
Both Ways	78
Christmas	79
Close to You	80
Coming to Terms With	81
Crossroads	82
Days of Future Past	83

Dear Sister	84
Diana Princess of Wales	85
Dreams in a Bottle	86
Faces	87
Fairy Tails	88
Father Time	89
Free Kuwait	90
Friends	91
Garden of My Life	92
Greed	93
Happiness	94
I Was There	95
Ireland	96
Is Anyone Out There	97
Jo	98
Johnny Palmer	99
Karen	100
Last Fight	101
Leader of the Pack	102
Lennon's Peace	103
Lifeboat	104
Love?	105
Maureen	106
Medical Intrusion	107
Missed	108
Misused Power	109
Moment in Time	110
My Best Gal	111
Nina's Story	112
Not Me	113
Now the Fighting is Over	114
Playing the Double	115
Poor	116
Questions	117
Ride the Rainbow	118
Riding High	119
Still Waiting	122
Streetwalker	123
Tell Me About the War Nan.	124

Title	Page
That Girl	125
That Handbag	126
The Babes of Tribulation	127
The Blackberry Man	128
The Bright Tomorrow	130
The Choice	131
The Craftsman	132
The Fighter	133
The Fox and the Clown	134
The Gap	136
The Gold Seeker	138
The Happy Ending	139
The Juvenile Delinquent	140
The Kiss	141
The Last Goodbye	142
The Legacy	143
The Miner	144
The Phoenix	145
The Sea	146
The Seafarer	147
The Silent Homecoming	148
The Soul Searcher	149
The Spell	150
The Wall	152
This Unholy War	153
Thomas And Jason 1998	154
Time {or The Lack of It}	155
Time {The Healer}	156
To Each His Own	157
Tomorrow is Another Day	158
Trains	159
What Have I Done	160
Will I Make the Grade	161
Willing to Learn	162
Would I	163
Yobs	164
You and Me	165

SNIPPETS

Snippets 1 169
Snippets 2 170
Snippets 3 171
Snippets 4 172
Snippets 5 173
Snippets 6 174
Snippets 7 175
Snippets 8 176
Snippets 9 177
Lucky Me 178

Introduction

I write about things that trouble me whether
It be cruelty to animals or conflicts of war.
I find sharing my thoughts with others has
Always been therapeutic. I'm not competent
And write mostly for friends who either say,
It made me laugh or it made me cry
Depending on the subject.
Is this a play on emotions I ask myself?

Rene McDermott

Animals

A Mouse Tale

The wind was cold and the snow came down,
And the five little mice all scurried around.
Where could they find some nice warm straw?
Or some extra food, they could do with more.

I have an idea said the daddy mouse,
I will go off and look for a comfy house.
We can squeeze down under the crack in the door,
And perhaps we can find some crumbs on the floor

The very next night as the cold wind blew,
He came back for mum and the little ones too.
I've found us a home he squealed with delight,
Where they leave out the biscuits and cheese every night.

At the back of the cupboard they settled with ease,
And when it was dark they came out for cheese.
But soon they would find that a shock was in store
As they left little mice dirt's all over the floor

Well, the cheese disappeared and the biscuits did too,
Locked up in the fridge with some cold Irish stew.
They hurried around from the front to the back,
Till they spotted a smelly piece set in a trap.

Hurray squealed the little ones, what have we here,
But daddy mouse cried, there is danger I fear.
We could take a chance, but I don't think its right,
The family comes first, so were leaving tonight.

Well, they all slipped away through the crack in the door,
They would find somewhere else that was safer for sure.
And though they were hungry and faced the cold weather,
The family survived and they all stayed together.

Animal Crackers

Be kind to animals, that's what you said
But the cat is upstairs fast asleep on my bed.
My tights that were dangling over the chair
Are riddled with claw marks and covered in hair.
He's prodded his paw in my jar of cold cream
And trod it all over my carpet of green.
And only last night he came in from the street
And plonked a half eaten dead mouse at my feet.

You also requested I clean out the rabbits
But didn't inform me of some of their habits.
In separate hutches they looked so forlorn
That I put them together and ten more were born.
They drop little currants all over the floor
And try to escape when I open the door.
If they breed any quicker I think I shall cry
Or shove the whole lot in a big rabbit pie.

And then there's the dog that lives next door but one
He comes in my garden and has lots of fun.
He's broke down my flowers and scratched up my seeds
And his urine just seems to encourage the weeds.
And while I was hanging my wash on the line
He sneaked in and pinched a pork chop that was mine.
They say he's got worms yet he doesn't get thinner
But I will if he keeps on nicking my dinner.

There's also the chickens outside in the pen
A bad tempered cock and a broody old hen.
When I take them their grit they just peck at my legs
And they never oblige with some nice new laid eggs.
The cock only crows when I'm having a kip
And the whole blooming lot really give me the pip.
Be nice to animals that's what you said
But I think I'll go jump in the river instead.

Big Bad Wolf

Who's afraid of the big bad wolf, why I said the mother hen,
He bit my legs and stole my eggs and then run off again.
Me too said Sam the little dog, he pulled out half my fur,
He ate my bone and chased me home and then went after her.
Poor Bess the cat looked very sad her tail was tattered and torn,
He drank my cream and made me scream as he dragged me across the lawn.
The tortoise lay there on his back, he cried, that wolf is shocking,
He turned me round here on the ground and left me here a rocking.
That's not too bad said the one eyed frog, I didn't see him arrive,
I turned too late and he'd ate my mate it's a miracle I'm alive.
What about me piped the little mouse, you all think you're in trouble,
But he squashed my knees and scoffed my cheese, now I can't squeak I just bubble.
Well I'm not afraid said the tiny flea, I can leave my worries behind me,
I have no fear I can bite his ear and he'll never know where to find me.
They all looked round at the tiny flea that was resting on the wall,
You're a brave wee thing we will make you king and the flea felt ten feet tall.
Then the wolf walked by with a baleful eye and the flea made ready to sting,
But he raised his paw, and the flea was no more, what a silly, silly Billy little king

They sing to herald the break of dawn,
They sing to wake me up in the morn.
They sing because they're happy and so they should be
Cos they've left all their mess, on my conservatory.
They sing to remind us that life's all around
And we don't always need both feet on the ground.
They sing to remind us that dreams can come true
Tho we aint born with wings, sometimes we can fly too.
But I'll clear up all their droppings it won't take too long,
It's a small price to pay for a song.

Dancing Bear

Help, where are they taking me, it seems a long long way,
My mothers always been with me, at least till yesterday.
But now I'm in a big black van and going who knows where,
A voice is saying I will make a fine young dancing bear.

Well now I've been unloaded and they have these red hot coals,
They make me stand upon them and the heat burns through my soles.
I have to hop and jump about my feet are really sore,
But all the men are clapping and there calling out for more.

They pierced my nose which really hurt and through it put a ring,
Then attached a length of rope which made my poor nose sting.
I realize that if I dance, they clap there hands with glee
And don't pull on the rope so hard, that's almost killing me.

So here I am upon the street performing for you all,
I cannot sit or lay me down; I have to stand up tall.
My life is filled with misery my pain beyond compare,
But in your eyes you only see, a fine young dancing bear.

Death of a Horse

Beautiful he was in all his glory,
As he trotted gaily down the London road.
Unaware of danger that was lurking,
And the bomb that any minute would explode.

His shiny coat was gleaming in the sunshine,
As he proudly kept in time with all the rest.
Yet soon he would be lying on the roadside,
With six inch nails embedded in his chest.

There was not any sign of pain impending,
As the blinding flashes brought him to the ground.
But suddenly his flesh was torn and bleeding,
As scraps of mangled metal flew around.

God knows how much he suffered in those moments,
Before the man approached him with a gun.
Yet, someone somewhere caused this bloody carnage,
That left him dying in the morning sun.

**ON JULY 20TH 1982, THE I.R.A.
CLAIMED RESPONSIBILITY FOR THE BOMB THAT EXPLODED,
KILLING AND MAIMING,
MEN AND HORSES OF THE HOUSEHOLD CAVELRY.**

Goldfish

Two little goldfish swimming in a pool
One said to the other one, I'm feeling such a fool.
I came here from a fairground where the atmosphere was gay
I learned to swim to music and to the beat I'd sway.
I'd do a little wiggle whenever Elvis sang and when tom Jones
Came bursting forth, I almost went off bang.
Dillon always made me dream and float around at random
Whilst Bassey made me flip a fin and writhe with gay abandon.
But here it's all so boring I find it all a drag
I wish I was back there again, inside that plastic bag.
So if you have a goldfish and you won it at the fair
Stand it by the radio and let the music blare.

Homeless

The orang-utan is loosing his home the forest is being chopped down,
A concrete jungle will take its place a barren and leafless town.
No hairy long arms will swing through the trees, no mating call sounds will we hear, the orang-utan wont have a place in the world and the species will soon disappear.

Leader of the Pack

I loved you Macarooni you were special from the start,
Although you chewed my plants and shoes, you crept into my heart.
You led the other dogs astray and taught then tricks of yours,
But only you could lead the way and open sliding doors.

I often called you baby and sometimes little friend,
I never knew how sick you were until the very end.
Your death has left me unprepared, my heart is full of tears,
But I thank you for the happiness you brought me through the years.

LOVE MUMMY

Scruffy

Scruffy was a funny dog, he didn't have a home,
He'd spend an hour with anyone who offered him a bone.
Not everybody loved him, some shoo'd him from the door,
But those who came to know him always called him back for more.
They loved the way he raised his paw and cocked his shaggy head,
And the thank you that shone in his eyes whenever he was fed.
The children all adored him, and one called Daisy May,
Had begged her mum to keep him when he followed her one day.
Her mother cried in horror what keep a dog like that,
No, you can have pedigree or else a Persian cat.
I wont, I wont, said Daisy May, acting very huffy,
I didn't want a dog at all it's just that I love Scruffy.
Well that is that, her mother said, now go on back to school,
What good's a silly dog like that, he's just no good at all.
Later on that same sad day as school came to a close,
Scruffy sat outside the gate and twitched his funny nose.
All the children patted him and watched him wag his tail,
But Daisy May just walked on by looking very pale.
If she couldn't have that silly dog and call him all her own,
She wouldn't make a fuss of him or take him to her home.
But as she crossed the busy road, the tears filled in her eyes,
And the driver of a big blue truck was taken by surprise.
He knew he couldn't brake in time no matter how he tried,
Then a dog ran out from nowhere and pushed the girl aside.
He felt the bump beneath his wheels, got out the cab with dread,
The girl had not a scratch or bruise, but Scruffy lay there dead.
Her mother soon came on the scene and said to Daisy May,
My darling, darling daughter, I have done you wrong today.
My tongue is very bitter, sharper than a knife,
I said that dog was little use and now he's saved your life.
He was buried in the garden and they came from far and wide,
To say goodbye to Scruffy and respect the way he died.
And Daisy May still talks to him until this very day,
She sits beside the flower beds and whiles an hour away.

Seals

Come with me my little one, I'll hide you out of reach,
For here's that nasty man again coming down the beach.
He's walking right towards us, a club within his hand,
I can't be with you any more, I hope you understand.
For somewhere in this cruel world, our skins are bought and sold,
It seems that people wear them, for keeping out the cold.
I can't see any reason why they should pick on us,
They have so much to choose from that's achieved with little fuss.
The sheep get hot in summer, and in order to keep cool,
It makes them very happy when shearers clip there wool.
And there's lots of man made fibres, that are super for the cold,
Whilst, you my little baby, are just a few days old.
So hide between these two fine rocks, and squeeze yourself down tight,
I'm hoping he will miss you if you stay clear out of sight.
And close your eyes my little one, I don't want you to see
The hand that lifts that cruel club and brings it down on me.
I don't want you to hear my cries, when stricken by his hand,
Or see my blood flow through the rocks and mingle with the sand.
I'm hoping you will stay alive, and somehow see the day,
When seals are left alone in peace, to live, and swim, and play.

The Badger Baiters

I hear their footsteps passing by my door,
I close my eyes as they go marching by.
I've seen the scene so many times before,
With dogs at heel and shovels carried high.

I know in which direction they will go,
To dig a pit, a prison for the pain.
I fight the tears that hide behind my eyes,
As the badger baiters make their move again.

What man can feast his eyes upon the scene,
And cheer as tender flesh is torn apart.
Can they watch the blood that freely flows,
Without the stain remaining on their heart.

No sweetness will be in my sleep tonight,
My dreams will not be gay or brightly lit.
My mind will feel the torment of the pain,
That rises from the darkness of the pit.

We cannot blame the dog that done the deed,
Or the erstwhile ones that fought and lost and ran.
For, though they tore the badger into shreds,
Their cruelty has been instilled by man.

The Day of the Animals

The animal kingdom is shaking with dread,
If things don't improve they will soon all be dead.
We are killing the foxes and hunting the deer,
And the rabbits breed well, but they still disappear.

We club little seals that are only just born,
And the rhino is slaughtered because of his horn.
There's young baby elephants dying of grief,
While their mother is slain by an ivory thief.

Badgers no longer are safe in their set,
We train dogs to fight to fulfil someone's bet.
Chemicals kill all that live in the soil,
And the fish and the birds are polluted with oil.

Cats have had fireworks tied to their tail,
The dolphin is dying and so is the whale.
Donkeys are tortured and left to their fate,
And monkeys transported packed tight in a crate.

Perhaps it is time that we started to think,
If we don't change our ways they will all be extinct.
Or, perhaps they will rise and decide on a plan,
To conquer the world, and their enemy, man.

The Foxes Lament

My heart is beating like a drum, my legs are getting tired,
I can't go on for very long although I'm well inspired.
I hear the hounds close on my trail, which fills me now with dread,
I know when they catch up with me they'll soon tear off my head.
But first I'll be tossed in the air and dragged along the ground,
My frightened eyes will clearly see the teeth of an angry hound.
I know I've been a naughty fox, a bit of fun I've had,
I've worried sheep and chickens too, but not been really bad.
If I just had a fighting chance, I'd face them now alone,
But I feel their breath upon my back, and I'm not nearly home.
The hole I go to ground in seems a million miles away,
There's nothing else that I can do, to keep those hounds at bay.
So my weary legs keep going, slipping in the mud,
Trying every trick I know to save my precious blood.
But now my chance is over, I know I have to die,
I just hope little foxes have a heaven in the sky.

The Lost Chance

Oh Billy you're a handsome goat
I've loved you for a while.
I still remember when we met
Twas there by yonder style.

Your horns were gleaming in the sun
A twinkle in your eye
I felt a bond tween me and you
The moment I passed by.

Ah nanny you're a sassy goat
You know that I've been smitten
I can't ignore you like I should
The love bugs truly bitten.

You have a wiggle when you walk
Your oozing sex appeal
But with this fence between us
I can't show you how I feel.

Oh Billy, jump the blinking fence
It shouldn't be too tricky
But wait, here comes another goat
His name is dodgy Dicky.

He's taken quite a shine to me
His ardour is intense
Perhaps it's better if you stay
Your own side of the fence.

Ah nanny you're a fickle one
You got me quite excited
If I had jumped the fence last night
You would have been delighted.

But he who hesitates is lost
I played it safe and waited
Now dodgy Dicky's done the deed
And I am left frustrated.

The moral of the story is
Don't keep them in suspense
To get the things you want in life
You have to jump the fence.

Vannie Gogh

Little friend you know how much I love you,
I rescued you when you were all alone.
Your frightened eyes were peeping from the hedgerow,
I scooped you up and took you to my home.

I never knew what cruelty befell you
Or how you came to only have one ear.
But soon you would be purring at the fireside,
Instead of shaking petrified with fear.

So many years we lived and played together,
You lay across my lap when I was sad.
Sometimes when the world was cold and lonely,
I felt that you were the only friend I had.

But now I see that weakness overcomes you,
I know your life is coming to an end,
The tears that fill my eyes will ease my heartache,
Till we meet in heaven little friend.

White Lies

Little Mo the rabbit was feeling very sad
His mother had been taken by a man he knew was bad.
All the other rabbit's, ran away in fear
And hid behind the hedgerow's whenever he came near.

But yesterday his mother was caught inside a trap
And he'd seen a man release her and put her in a sack.
Poor Mo had felt so helpless as he shivered out of sight
And the thought of what became of her had made him cry all night.

He asked his other rabbit friends but they all turned away
It seemed that even if they knew, they weren't prepared to say.
I know, he thought I'll see the owl, they say he's very wise
He will not turn his back on me or fob me off with lies.

So off into the woods he went and found the tallest tree
But the owl just looked at little mo and said repeatedly.
I really think its better that you should never know
I would not like to tell you, so I think you ought to go.

But little mo insisted so the owl began to speak
He told of a laboratory that lay behind the creek.
Lots of different animals were gathered in that place
Where experiments are carried out to help the human race.

But will they hurt my mother enquired little mo
She's soft and warm and fluffy and I really love her so.
I couldn't bear it if I thought she suffered any pain
But if you tell me honestly I'll be at peace again.

The owl in all his wisdom, turned his head away
It wouldn't serve a purpose to tell the truth today.
You mustn't worry little Mo, your mother is all right
And that of course is how a lie, can be described as white.

Humour

Annabelle Jane

This is the story of Annabelle Jane, who piddled her knickers again and again.
She went in a café and ordered a tea but before it arrived she was dying to pee.
So spotting the ladies she started to rise but then to the on looking waiters surprise.
Instead of proceeding to walk over there she piddled a puddle all over the chair.
It soon overflowed and run down on the floor all steamy and sliding right up to the door.
And then to his horror he heard the girl mutter, if you open the door it will run in the gutter.
I can't he exclaimed, for it just isn't proper to open the door that now acts as a stopper.
Just think of those passing and carrying shopping they'll paddle in piddle and get their feet sopping.
And if they slip over and fall on their faces they'll end up with urine in very strange places.
Instead I will fetch you a bucket and mop and I'll pour disinfectant all over the shop.
So Annabelle started to take off her knickers that smelt like a carton of fortnight old kippers.
And seeing the waiter had gone for the bucket she shook them around then murmured, oh suck it.
I won't get them dry if I squeeze them or shove them so she popped them inside the new microwave oven.
In less than a minute they'd dried up so much that a dirty great scorch mark appeared on the crutch.
The elastic had melted and gone kind of rotten but still they felt lovely and warm on her bottom.
By this time the waiter had brought what was needed so taking the bucket and mop she proceeded.
To clean up the mess with incredible speed but before she had finished, again she had peed.

It poured down her legs like a fast flowing stream while the waiter began to hysterically scream.
Your blooming disgusting, you've done it again and he snatched the wet mop from Annabelle Jane.
Get out he cried as he showed her the door but then he slipped up on the soaking wet floor.
Annabelle giggled then looked in surprise, why!! Could that be hatred she saw in his eyes.
Why was he laying there like a drowned pup making no effort to pick himself up.
Get out he spluttered, walk out of the door I don't want to see you in here any more.
But how could she leave when she couldn't get past, you'll just have to move she informed him at last.
I can't move a muscle he hissed through his teeth I won't move an inch till your out on the street.
Well I'll have to step over said Annabelle Jane but as she was trying it happened again.
You're filthy he cried then proceeded to choke as the puddle she piddled ran all down his throat.
I'm terribly sorry she said with a grin it's a terrible, terrible state you are in.
I'm glad I am leaving, I wouldn't drink tea, served by a waiter all covered in pee.

Bags

There's plastic bags and paper bags that advertise
Bags to carry shopping in of every shape and size.

Jiffy bags and snappy bags and bags for walnut whips
Bags to carry laundry in and some for fish and chips.

Bags the postman carries to bring around your bills
And little ones on aeroplanes a queasy flyer fills.

But most of all my favourites are big black dustbin bags
You use them for so many things you're washing or your rags.

And if you find you need a dress they can look really smashing
whichever way you wear them they will be the height of fashion.

What's more when you return at night all weary and done in
You needn't bother to undress; you just jump in the bin.

Be Mine

Note the way my fingers tremble as you count your crispy pounds
How my ears prick up and listen to your silvers clinking sounds.
See my eyes begin to sparkle looking at your golden chain
The way I nestle in your Bentley trying not to look too vain.
Watch my toes turn up and outward as you stand in evening dress
How I shiver when you purchase with American express.
No, of course it's not your money that has made the love light shine
More the thought that if we marry, all your riches will be mine.

Cack-Handed Kate

This is the story of cack-handed Kate
Who spent all her life in pursuit of a mate.
At sixteen she fancied the boy from next door
And joined him to dance on the school ballroom floor.

She waltzed like a princess but then made a slip
And her earring got caught on his brass trouser zip.
She tried to unhook it while down on her knees
But he started to sweat like a mouldy old cheese.

Just take off your earring he growled through tight lips
So she tugged and his trousers came down off his hips.
You great stupid moron he shouted at Kate
Then stepped from his pants in a smouldering state.

As his thin bony legs made it out of the door
With inelegant ease Kate got up from the floor.
I guess he don't like me, to leave me stood here
With his trousers a dangling down from my ear.

Years later a fella named reg caught her eye
And she bought him a scarf and a bright yellow tie.
She told him to wear it and asked him to tea
And fed him boiled eggs as she sat on his knee.

The undercooked eggs dribbled all down his chin
And she mopped it all up with a rag soaked in gin.
He made his excuse and ran out the door
And she never saw reg or his tie anymore.

At forty she fell for a much older guy
Who didn't like sex but she urged him to try.
She slipped in his room and crawled under the sheet
Then she discovered he'd died in his sleep.

Cheer Up

Hey, you with the long and miserable face,
And the burden that weighs a ton.
Have you got woodworm in a wooden leg,
or a pimple on your bum.
Have you got children sick with disease,
That can't be cured with care.
Are they crying with hunger pains,
While your cupboard is empty bear.
Have you a nose like Pinocchio,
Or ears that flap in the breeze.
Are you so rusty and terribly old,
That you cannot bend at the knees.
Have you a house that is tumbling down,
With nothing to take it's place.
Do people laugh and point at you,
Cause you've such a peculiar face.
Haven't you got a friend in the world,
Who you'd tell your troubles to.
Has someone said you'd look more at home,
In a cage at the London zoo.
If none of these things apply to you,
But you still feel sad and glum.
Then all I can say is the best you deserve,
Is that pimple on your bum.

Diamonds are Forever

Note the way my fingers tremble, as you count your crispy pounds,
How my ears prick up and listen, to your silver clinking sounds.
See my eyes begin to sparkle, looking at your golden chain,
The way I nestle in your Bentley, trying not to look to vain.

Watch my toes turn out and upwards, as you stand in evening dress,
How I shiver when you purchase, with American express.
No, of course it's not your money, that has made the lovelight shine,
More the thought, that if we marry, all your riches will be mine.

Feed Me

I could do with some fried green tomatoes,
And some strawberry ice cream in my tea.
I would eat mustard sauce, off a pox ridden horse,
And it still wouldn't satisfy me.

Cos I've been on a diet since Monday,
And my temper is wearing quite thin.
My longing for food makes me tetchy and rude,
And I'm dribbling all down my chin.

So give me some roast beef and gravy,
Or kippers and custard with jam.
A haggis with honey a fur coated bunny,
A pie filled with scrag end of lamb.

I'd devour a can full of maggots,
Or the entrails that came from a rat.
I'm not really greedy but please someone feed me,
I'd rather be happy and fat.

Gooday

I haven't got a lot to do
So how about if me and you
Pay a visit to the zoo
You pay

After we will stroll around
See the buildings in the town
Find a bench and settle down
I'll pay

By then we'll want a tasty meal
Plump pink prawns and tender veal
Chocolate cakes with cream that's real
You pay

And then we'll walk around the park
Cuddle up until it's dark
Carve our names into the bark
I'll pay

What's this you don't seem very keen
Why are you saying I am mean
And that my little game you've seen
I say

I worked it out with lots of care
To make sure we both paid our share
What ! Change them over that's not fair
No way

I Want

I'd like to have a great big shed with lots and lots of room
Where I could store my bits and bobs the hoover and the broom.

I'd like it slightly heated so in the winter time
My plants could all be stored away until the weathers fine.

I wouldn't have to throw away the things I like to hoard
I'd always find a cardboard box some tissues or some card.

I'd also like a bathroom door that when you pushed it too
Would stay shut for the moment that I did what I must do.

But it always swings back open and no one gets a treat
To see me sitting on the loo my knickers round my feet.

Just A Girl

I'd like to be a little boy
A dinkle in my trousers
I'd be the leader of the gang
They call the rebel rousers.

I'd play with cars and fire guns
And tie things up with cable
I'd buy a tool set of my own
And chop legs off the table.

Alas, I'm just a little girl
All sweet, clean and quiet
But wait until I reach sixteen
Boy, then I'll cause a riot.

Marie

There she sat in all her glory
On the television screen
Long blond hair and eyes a shining
Telling how her life had been.

Ah, I felt so sympathetic
So much so I almost cried
How could someone so vivacious
Feel so lonely deep inside.

Gosh! There must be men a plenty
Queuing up to share her life
With her nature strong, but gentle
She would make a super wife.

Then I saw a little twinkle
In those eyes that seemed so sad
It was kilroy she was after
Boy! She fancied him like mad.

I bet the filming barely finished
When she grabbed him by the bum
Now his hair has gone completely
And he's shrunk to five foot one.

Naughty

I stole a piece of heather that adorned a garden wall
I called out hello lofty to a guy of six foot tall.
I sniggered when a schoolboy slipped up on the ice
And teased my friend who had a boil which wasn't very nice.
I filled an empty bottle up and labelled it as gin
And just to tempt the dustmen I left it by the bin.
The postman got his fingers caught delivering the mail
It only opened half an inch I'd jammed it with a nail.
And then the poor old milkman became a bit confused
He couldn't pick the bottles up I'd stuck them down with glue.
I loudly called out tea up to some workmen in the street
Then hid around the corner while they stamped their angry feet.
So it's not the ring confidence that hovers round my lip
It's because I've been a naughty girl and let my halo slip.

Never Judge a Book by It's Cover

They always called him Droopy Don, for everything drooped down
Beneath his brow his eyelids seemed to sag.
His mouth drooped at the corners and he wore a droopy hat
And his overcoat hung limply like a rag.

But one day Elsie Knockemback came looking for a job
As Droopy Don was busy making hay.
I beg you sir she pleaded, I'm the best you'll ever find
I'm the kind of girl that likes to earn her pay.

Beneath his droopy eyelids he surveyed her wicked form
All in and out like valleys hills and dales.
Her legs were strong like tree trunks her hips were broad and wide
Her breasts stood out like mammoth milking pails.

I'll take you on said Droopy Don you look a fine young wench
I guess that you could plough a field or two.
Also when the nights are drawing in and all the hay is stacked
I'm sure to find you something else to do.

The village people gathered round to watch them in the field
Bert Dangle said I can't believe his luck.
Handsome young tom randy muttered through his gritted teeth
She's the kind of chicken I would like to pluck.

Back down in the local they took bets on who would score
Even Jimmy Gay joined in the fun.
With Ivor Harden favourite and Bill Bonk running close
With little Jimmy Virgin ten to one.

The summer days grew shorter and the hay was neatly stacked
And Elsie was invited to the dance.
She must have been frustrated stuck up there with Droopy Don
So tonight the boys were all in with a chance.

The barn was over flowing and the was in full swing
When Droopy Don brought Elsie through the door.
Tom Randy made a bee line with Bert Dingle on his heels
But Ivor Harden dragged her on the floor.

He whirled her round the dance hall like a man who won a prize
While Billy bonk stood begging for a turn.
He felt her milk pails wobble as they rested on his chest
As his thighs began to sizzle up and burn.

You're going to get a treat tonight he whispered in his ear
I think we'd better take a walk out side.
But Elsie only laughed at him and pulled herself away
I don't need anything from you she cried.

I've been up at the farmhouse now for six or seven weeks
I know you call my govnor droopy don.
But you have only seen him in his mac and floppy hat
While I have seen him stripped with nothing on.

We've made love on the tables we've made love on the chairs
We've even had a muff dive from the shelf.
I've had a lot of men before but never one like him
So go away and make love to yourself.

Well she left the dance that evening on the arm of droopy don
While the others scuttled off like scalded cats.
But from that time the local lads have changed their style of dress
And the village shop is selling floppy hats.

Perhaps the law of gravity has gone right up the creek
No longer is it that what goes up comes down.
But if you leave things dangling that can't be put to use
You may have the finest working part in town.

Nit Wit

A nit lay on a strand of hair knowing soon he'd be
Not just a dull and useless nit, but a fine and active flea.
He'd bite and sting and leap about and find himself a wife
He loved this head he nestled in and planned to stay for life.
But, what's this here some nasty teeth on the end of a cruel comb were
trying hard to scratch him out and move him from his home.
But try as they might he wouldn't budge the hair he stuck to fast
And ages later so it seemed, the comb gave up at last.
Ah ha he laughed I dodged it well it couldn't get to me
And as he shook with merriment, he turned into a flea.
He bit and stung and leapt and jumped and then the comb came back
But this time he could not escape, crrrrrrrrack.

No Will Power

I've tried to pack up smoking, so many times before,
but every time I cut it down, I end up smoking more.

I hate those dirty ash trays, the smudges on my clothes,
The way the smoke gets in my eyes, and sometimes up my nose.

I've listened to the sayings, like, "if you were meant to smoke,
There would be a chimney on your head, to see you didn't choke".

But my breath is getting shorter, and I find it hard to run,
Yet even while I puff and pant, I light another one.

I'm sure I'm not a weakling, I'll kick the habit yet,
But while I think up how it's done, I'll smoke a cigarette.

Poor Little Rich Girl

Poor little rich girl it seems to me
You're badly in need of sympathy.
You can't make your mind up what dress to wear
Or how many diamonds to put in your hair.
You've so many invites to parties and things
That increase every time that the telephone rings.
Your cook slaves for hours preparing a meal
But you have to choose if it's lobster or veal.
Good looking men that are oozing with charm
Fight to protect you and keep you from harm.

Ah poor little rich girl you don't know the bliss
Of newspapers wrapped around cold greasy fish.
Or draughty old trains that go under the ground
And buses that run if their not broken down.
You don't carry shopping until your arms break
And nobody shouts if you make a mistake.
You've not had the pleasure of joining a queue
Ah poor little rich girl ------ I wish I were you.

Scandals

I've never been one for repeating a tale
A secret is sacred with me.
But I must tell some things I heard this week
While we sit with our biscuits and tea.

There's Jenny McGraw who went out Friday night
In an outfit more shocking than naughty.
She was seen with a man barely twenty years old
While she is the wrong side of forty.

I hear that old Jimmy who lives down the lane
Has been lurking down by the sewer.
If his turnips are bigger than ever this year
We will know where he got his manure.

Then there is busted Bessie's wee boy
She insists he's the sole of perfection.
But I bet he gets caught pinching sweets from the shop
And ends up in the school of correction.

Well, what do you think of the Corrigan twins
They both bunk off school on the quiet.
While Billy the boy who lives next door but one
Was in court for inciting a riot.

Mrs Whites husband has left her you know
She says he's working in Cairo.
But I think he ran off with the post office blond
That he met when he cashed in his giro.

Ah well I must go, I've got shopping to do
and I want to avoid Rita Randal.
She runs down her neighbours and even her friends
I, can't abide gossip or scandal.

Sharing

I remember Tommy Stone when we were little boys
I used to let him wear my clothes and play with all my toys
He didn't have a father and his mum was on the gin
And when I saw him shake with cold I used to ask him in
He used to sit and gaze at me with eyes of velvet brown
Whilst promising to be my friend and never let me down
We'd scoff my mother's cookies and sip at mugs of tea
Yet secretly I gloated for I knew he envied me.

But what a lot can happen within the hands of time
For now he's getting married to a girl who once was mine
His suits all come from Savil Row he drives a limousine
And yet I'm sure he doesn't work his nails are much too clean
He came to pay a visit about a year ago
I introduced him to my girl which only goes to show
That if you have a special girl you keep her for your own
For now I'm filled with envy 'cause I shared with Tommy Stone.

Speed Freak

Speeding up the motorway at 80 miles an hour
Exhilaration fills me as I glory in the power.
Passing little mini cars whose drivers are insane
To be content with dawdling along the inside lane.
Now I'm doing 90 and "wow "I'm having fun
Put my foot down harder and hit the magic ton.
It's the only way to travel keeps running through my head
Then comes that feared explosive sound that drivers always dread.
The wheel was torn beneath my grasp the car began to swerve
A centre reservation loomed and then I lost my nerve.
Among the tangled wreckage I gave an anguished groan
And heard a voice cry franticly, the tyre must have blown.
Lights were flashing everywhere when through a crack I saw
The row of little mini cars I overtook before.
As they slowly passed me by they gazed with sympathy
For they'd be safely home again before I was cut free.
So if I live to tell the tail and ever drive again
I'll join those little mini cars along the inside lane.

Temptation

Why are you enticing me, you naughty, naughty man
You know I never could resist a lovely golden tan.
I know your reputation, is to kiss the girls and run
And a girl expects a whole lot more when all is said and done.

So, take me to the cracker factory, let me go insane
I never want to hear your voice or see your face again.
But just before I take my leave and you go on your way,
Lets have some slap and tickle and a quick roll in the hay.

The Diet

I looked into the mirror and boy did I look fat,
I grabbed a lump of flesh and thought I must get rid of that.
I didn't want to wobble whilst walking up the town,
And feel those rolls of flabby flesh bobbling up and down.
And so I chose my diet and started it that day,
I nibbled at a lettuce leaf and hid the bread away.
I managed well from breakfast time right on up till noon,
Dreaming of a slim and lovely body I'd have soon.
But when it got to one-o-clock my thoughts began to alter,
I dreamed of drinking lemonade instead of water.
I visualized a fat pork chop and lovely golden chips,
But settled for a carrot that was kinder to my hips.
And then spread some cottage cheese upon a dry ryvita,
Whilst trying to convince myself I was a tiny eater.
By four-o-clock my hunger was more than I could bear,
So I thought I'd cheat a little bit and scoff a juicy pear.
I really did enjoy it as the juice ran down my chin,
I gobbled up each tasty bit the pips, core and skin.
So then I thought I'd work it off and go and clean the car,
But resting on the dashboard was a milky chocolate bar.
Oh goodness what temptation it really wasn't fair,
Bur surely it could not hurt much if I just ate one square.
By ten-o-clock the chocolate was gone I gazed down at my hips,
Ah well they didn't look so bad I'd buy some fish and chips.
And though I hadn't done too well I didn't feel much sorrow,
I told myself it wouldn't hurt I'd start again tomorrow.

The Flight

I'm not light on my feet and an aeroplane seat
Is not quite as wide as my bottom.
Well I know with my luck I am bound to get stuck
And the incident wont be forgotten.
My friends will all chuckle as I fight with the buckle
Of a seat belt that wont even meet.
The steward won't smile if I'm stuck in the aisle
With his trolley jammed up by my feet.

So I'm going to slim and it's not just a whim
I've been meaning to do it for ages.
I will forfeit my dinner to get myself thinner
And buy cottage cheese with my wages.
By this time next year you won't know me I fear
As I lie on the beach in Marbella.
With a nice golden tan I will get me a man
And I won't hide beneath an umbrella.

But just for today well I guess its okay
To have crackers and cheese with my beers.
I will give myself treats and eat cream cakes and sweets
Till the chocolate runs out of my ears.
So if in a while I am destined to smile
At a man who prefers chunky women.
I'll be happy right here sitting on Brighton pier
And I won't give a toss about slimming.

The Frog's Lament

Jumping here and jumping there
Little frog's legs everywhere.
What's the panic all about
That man has got the mower out.

He's going to drive us all away
Our habitat will go today.
If we don't leave this nice long grass
Our bodies will be cut in half.

So hop it mister, leave us be
Go in and have a cup of tea.
You build a pond so we may spawn
And now our playgrounds on the lawn.

But soon it's hibernation time
We sleep below the mud and slime.
We won't be there to hop about
And you can get the mower out.

So give us chance to hide away
You needn't cut the grass today.
Just leave the mower in the shed
We can't eat greenfly if we're dead.

The Old Days

They eyed each other warily, two old and wrinkled men,
Then one called to the other one, "I say is your name Len"?
Did you go to school with me back in our younger days,
And did you keep a small white mouse to frighten mother Hayes.
Gawd love us! Why it's Harry Pimm, a snide I do recall,
Ah yes, well I remember you back in our days at school.
You lifted up the teachers desk and hid my mouse inside,
And when she screamed and ran away you laughed until you cried.
But not content with doing that, you wouldn't take the blame,
You told her that the mouse was mine, and I received the cane.
It serves you right said Harry Pimm, you pulled a stroke on me,
You wrote rude things on the lavvy wall for all the boys to see.
And then you spread the rumour round you'd seen me coming out,
And teacher grabbed me by the ear and gave me such a clout.
Len threw his hat upon the floor and scratched his balding head,
He cried, well bless my cotton socks! That wasn't what I said.
But if you think I snitched on you we'll have it out right here,
Roll up your sleeves you dirty rat while I put down my beer.

Well, you should have seen them shaping up, two men of eighty four,
Settling an age old grudge of seventy years or more.
Then another stepped between them, why! Isn't it Sidney Green,
Wasn't you teachers pet, all snooty, smart and clean.
Why yes, he said, but to this day I've always bore the shame,
Twas me you see who hid the mouse and didn't take the blame.
I hated being teachers pet while you had all the fun,
That's why I wrote on the lavvy wall, I did it quick, then run.
They grabbed him by his tatty coat that dangled at the hem,
I'll break your neck said Harry Pimm, I'll cripple you said Len.
Please don't do that, poor Sidney cried, the deed is long since done,
I'll buy you both a pint of beer if I can be your chum.
What!! A pint of beer off Sidney Green that snooty little horror,
But a pint of beer's a pint of beer, we'll bash him up tomorrow.

The Place to Be

Old farmer Rumble was having his tea,
When his wife plonked her twenty five stone on his knee.
"Sam Rumble" she said, "it's been ten years or more,
Since we had a french kiss and made love on the floor".

He choked on his sausage, then to his wife Meg,
He cried, "get off woman, your breaking my leg".
"I haven't got time to be randy or frisky,
My backs playing up and it's too blooming risky".

"oh, come on" cried Meg, "I can jump on the top,
And if your in trouble I promise to stop".
"the cows in the meadow, the sheep's in the fold,
So take off your trousers and do as your told".

Sam took a deep breath and with all of his might,
Pushed Meg on to the floor, what a orrible sight
She looked like her body was pumped up with air,
As she lay in a heap at the foot of his chair.

"what's up with you woman" cried Sam in dismay,
"I've had my right arm up a cows bum to-day".
"I was up at five thirty collecting the eggs, and the donkey got randy and
peed on my legs".

"that's alright", said Meg, "I don't care if your mucky,
If you play your cards right you will really get lucky".
"I'm turned on by fingernails grimed up with dirt,
And the smell of manure that clings to your shirt".

Then she grabbed at his legs as he made his escape,
And his heels sprouted wings as he made for the gate.
He could hear her voice calling behind the front door,
As she lifted her twenty five stone from the floor.

Sam took a deep breath and went on down the lane,
He would soon see the face that he loved once again.
She put Meg to shame with her big soulful eyes,
And the lovely firm flesh that surrounded her thighs.

In the meadow he spotted the love of his life,
What a beauty she was, not a bit like his wife.
Sam had a bad day but he's quite happy now,
As he gazes with love at his prize Jersey cow.

The Star

The papers say she's fifty two, but I know that's a lie,
According to my reckoning, she must be fifty five.
Yet there she posed upon the stage, a vision dressed in pink,
Not a wrinkle anywhere it made me stop and think.

No one on that crowded stage could put her looks to shame,
The others all looked dowdy, uninteresting and plain.
And as the camera focused on that flawless perfect face,
The hands of time disintegrated, lost without a trace.

God ! I thought, it isn't fair, whatever does she do,
Can that beauty be achieved with just a tuck or two.
And come to that what does she eat, her figures so divine,
Unlike those lumps of surplus fat that hang all over mine.

Zoom that camera in again, there must be like as not,
A laughter line, a tiny scar, a pimple or a spot.
It can't be true I tell myself, it's just a wicked trick,
But, not one imperfection shows, it really makes me sick.

Perhaps when she is on her own and toddles off to bed,
Her teeth go in a china jar, her wig comes off her head.
Without her bra to give support, her boobs drop to her knee.
And when she scrapes her makeup off, I bet she looks like me.

The Sun Dodger

I went down to Brighton on Sunday; the weather was 90 degrees,
I put on a very long t shirt and wore wellie boots up to my knees.
I knew that I mustn't get sunburn, for my dial a ride job was at stake,
So I added some extra long bloomers to make sure my skin didn't flake.

Then I covered my face with some netting so my nose wouldn't burn and get red.
I wore gloves that came up to my elbows and a dirty great hat on my head,
Well I gingerly stepped into the water and was several feet out very soon,
But the water got into my bloomers and I swelled like a barrage balloon.

Before I could gather my senses a boat full of people pulled near,
They were clicking away with their cameras and I started to wobble with fear.
They were shouting we've captured a monster and they hauled me aboard in a net,
The way that they prodded and poked me is a feeling I'd rather forget.

But I wriggled and struggled like crazy till they finally let me explain,
That I had to be white as a lily to be able to drive once again,
Well they thought I was telling a story and their attitude filled me with fear,
For they made me their prize exhibition, I'm on show each day on the pier.

The Worried Egg

I'm sitting here in someone's hand
I guess my time is up,
Will I be a soft boiled egg
That sits inside a cup.
Or will they gently poach me
Three minutes at the most,
Or maybe they will scramble me
And serve me up on toast.

I might be fried in cooking oil
Or whisked up in a cake,
Or end up in a custard tart
That someone's going to bake.
I could be steamed or coddled
Or sliced up on a stick,
But I'd rather I was fertilized
And came out as a chick.

Traffic Wardens

Ugh, I really hate them, with their yucky yellow bands,
I'd like to take their scrawny necks, and squeeze them in my hands.

No matter where I park my car, they always seem to pick it,
And smirking like a Cheshire cat they write me out a ticket.

I feed the parking meters, with ten pence, sometimes two,
Yet even though I hurry back, it's always over due

And underneath the wipers like a flipping paper flag,
Is stuffed the excess charge sheet, in a see through plastic bag

I'm cursed by traffic wardens, they follow me I think,
If only they would vanish, or at least run out of ink

But I bet they crawl beneath my car and paint on yellow lines,
As I pop round to the post box to mail my parking fines

What Matters Most

I know my spellings pretty poor, I guess I'm not too bright,
And though I use a dictionary, I still don't get it right.
I could have been a journalist and done the job quite well,
Or I might have been prime minister, if only I could spell.

But I couldn't join the forces, I'd be banished from the ranks,
I'm what they call a "dick ed" I'm as thick as two short planks.
The "old bill" wouldn't want me, for imagine my report,
"i chaasd im wiv me trunchen, an e swor wen e was cort".

But when I went to school you see our country was at war,
We only did an hour or two, not nine o-clock to four.
The teachers were inadequate, no educational toys,
I was mostly down the shelters making whoopee with the boys.

So my brain was left in limbo, not too sure what I should do,
Tho my air raid shelter training taught me quite a thing or two.
I would like to say with honesty, at sex I could excel,
But, I laid and thought of England, so I failed at that as well.

But I lived life in the fast lane, and threw a real mean dart,
I learnt to be good mannered, well, at least I didn't fart.
And I learned to practice peace and love and lend a helping hand,
And I learned to listen to my friends and tried to understand.

I also learned compassion for all creatures great and small,
And I learned to pick the pieces up whenever I should fall.
And I learned how to be happy, and I learned that lesson well,
So that is why, I never found the time to learn to spell.

White and Wong

White and Wong were like no others
They were very different brothers
One was short and one was tall
White was bright and Wong a fool

Every night they had their dinner
One got fat and one got thinner
One went early up to bed
The other sat up late and read

In the morning it would seem
That both had, had a different dream
So one was happy one was sad
One felt good the other bad

White drank coffee from a cup
And always done the washing up
But Wong preferred a stronger drink
And left his glasses in the sink

Why Do Things Always Go Wrong

I went for a drink with my boyfriend
And jumped up to sing him a song
But I felt such a clown for the mic had broke down
Oh why do things always go wrong.

I decided to ask him to dinner
To prove that my cooking was able
But the meat was half raw and it slid on the floor
As I carried the plates to the table.

So I asked him to sample my pastry
And hoped that it wasn't too hard
I soon had my proof when he broke his front tooth
And the rest of it had to discard.

When he took me to visit his mother
I put on my prettiest dress
But it poured down with rain and I tripped on a drain
And arrived in a terrible mess.

On the day that we went to the races
He asked me to put on his bet
But I backed the wrong horse and it run off the course
And it hasn't gone past the post yet.

Then he offered to help with my garden
And he shifted a whole pile of dirt
But I turned with the hose and aimed straight at his nose
And the water run all down his shirt.

Well I told him I'd like to get married
And he said that we could before long
But he hasn't been near not for more than a year
Oh why do things always go wrong.

From The Heart

A Day in the Life of Misfortune

No more tears are left to cry
Can she breathe another sigh
Why does good luck pass her by
Poor Linda

Always dealt the cards out fair
Gave her friendships loving care
I find her pain so hard to bear
Oh Linda

Yet I know there'll be a time
When the sun is bound to shine
And everything will turn out fine
For Linda

Her suffering won't be in vain
For as the rainbow follows rain
My darling will rejoice again
Dear Linda

Always

Stay with me when spring is nigh and daffodils wave golden heads in splendour,
And when I feel dejected and the words I speak are often less than tender.

Stay with me through summer, when the melting sun brings forth the hot and sultry nights. And when my tempers short because my legs are red and burnt and full of insect bites.

Stay with me in autumn when the leaves drift down like butterflies with broken wings. While I complain that nights are drawing in and I have failed to do a million things.

Stay with me in winter when the cold translucent icicles shine diamond bright. And hold me in your arms until the fire in my heart ignites our love and warms us gently through the night.

Stay with me forever.

Alzheimers

In your eyes I found warmth to cheer me through a winter's day.
In your eyes I saw a light to lead me when I lost my way.
In your eyes I saw your soul and gave you mine in sweet return.
In your eyes I traded dreams and watched the passion wildly burn.

In your eyes no longer now a recognition do I see.
In your eyes a vacant stare no tenderness shines down on me.
In your eyes the passing years have crystallised the youthful dew.
Yet in my eyes I pray you see reflections of my love for you.

Balance of Poverty

Some people said the other day, our lives are pretty grim
We guess we get enough to eat, were not exactly thin.
We've got a television and the house is not too cold
And we even run a little car although it's fairly old.

But we find that life's a struggle and feel we should have more,
We've always worked, scrimped and saved yet still we end up poor.
Were fed up with this country who's leader is a bitch
If only she'd retire, we could all get nice and rich.

Well! I thought about these people, who said that life was tough
And I guess that anything they had would never be enough.
I would like to take them on a trip to places on this earth
Cambodia, el Salvador where life's of little worth.

I would make them watch the children who were lacking food and homes,
Whose belly swelled with hunger and skin hung on their bones.
No comfy beds, no crusty rolls, no cakes or apple pies
Just sickness starvation, squalor, filth and flies.

Romania we'd visit next a place where tyrants rule,
Where no one ever speaks their mind they teach them that at school.
Where men are shot at random and women queue for bread
And orphans squat with tear filled eyes, among the sick and dead.

Then, off to Nicaragua where children wonder why
The government have stolen all and left them there to die.
They stretch there little fingers out to reach a grain of rice
And then the old grim reaper comes, and takes away their life.

These are the situations, which should haunt us every day
As we suffer from self pity and complain about the pay.
We are blessed with great advantage that's denied too many more
So, if you live in England please don't tell me you are poor.

Beyond the Vine

In the splendour of the evening
When the stars are in the sky.
Does your life spread out before you
Like a sheet hung out to dry.

Are there times of gentle breezes
Reminisce of childhood years.
Do you still recall the tender
Hands that wiped away your tears.

And when stormy clouds are raging
Do you stand with head held high.
Facing life with faith and courage
Even though you want to cry.

Can you walk into the sunlight
Knowing in your heart its true.
That you spared a thought for others
any time they needed you.

Do you treasure happy moments
So much more than gain or wealth.
If it's so, then my friend Vicky
You are true unto yourself.

Both Ways

I cannot see what you can see, or feel what you can feel,
There is no way for me to tell if tears are false or real.

You tell me that you love me, but how can I be sure,
You may be wanting someone else, and finding me a bore.

Nor, can I know if you are true each time we are apart,
For I cannot see inside your head, or climb inside your heart.

And who am I to say that what I see shine in your eyes,
Is love and deep affection, and not just clever lies.

I can't be sure of anything, there is no guarantee,
But, then love, on the other hand, you can't be sure of me.

Christmas

Tasty turkey, Christmas pudding
Lights that sparkle on the tree.
Gift wrapped presents in the corner
Some for you and some for me.
Sipping drinks from fancy glasses
Feeling good and warm inside.
Greeting friends and pulling crackers
We are blessed this Christmastide.
But what about the sad and lonely
Those who's pain is hard to bear.
Counting hours slowly passing
Staring at an empty chair.
Nose pushed up against the window
Watch the world go passing by.
Hearing sounds of distant laughter
Chocking on an anguished cry.
So let us pause for one brief moment
While we shed a silent tear.
For all the souls in need of comfort
Now that Christmas time is here.

Close to You

Can you see me when you close your eyes,
Pray tell the truth don't fob me off with lies.
Am I with you when your on your own,
My presence felt although you were alone.

Can you feel me when I'm far away,
And hear the words, the ones I always say.
If we can touch although we are apart,
Then I will live forever in your heart.

Coming to Terms With

Through all the pain and agony of youth
I tried to find some answers to this life
But never was I given any proof
The world was not a base for war and strife.

As nations fought to conquer and control
And hunger gnawed in far off distant lands
I felt that I should play a leading role
And hold the key to justice in my hands.

So many times the tears ran down my cheeks
As I fought lost causes time and time again
With restlessness invading on my sleep
Frustrations almost rendered me insane.

But as the years have passed it's been made clear
I cannot change the face of destiny
For that is not the reason I am here
The world can not be put to right by me.

I'm one of many cogs within a wheel
Designed to play a very tiny part
But even so I make my presence real
By caring for those nearest to my heart.

Crossroads

Imagine that you're on this path to nowhere,
A place that you might stay a long, long time.
The road begins to fork in two directions
And on each side you read a warning sign.

One tells you that the road is cold and lonely,
Although you may find shelter on the way.
But often you will feel quite unprotected,
As darkness comes to steal the light of day.

The other has a surface hard to master,
Jagged cruel rocks and shifting sand.
But someone will be there to walk beside you,
And offer you the comfort of a hand.

Whichever road you choose could lead to danger,
The shelters may be few and far between.
The hand can't guarantee to lead you safely,
For many things in life remain unseen.

So as you stand and ponder your decision,
Torn between the perils and the pain.
Remember, if you choose and fail the distance,
Someday you'll reach a crossroads once again.

Days of Future Past

Crazy lady, seek not for your sanity
Nor let confusion wander from your mind
Why delve into the past for stark reality
You may deplore the pictures that you find

The muffled noises spinning round inside your head
Dismiss the anguished screams of days gone by
And agonies increase when they are daily fed
Far better that they wither up and die.

Ne'er brush away the cobwebs clouding o'er your brain
Nor let the garbled words be understood
Tis easier to peacefully be thought insane
Than bowing to conventions cross of wood.

Retain the make believe that spells simplicity
And cultivate the simple smile to last
To live within yourself must be you destiny
Protected in the days of future past.

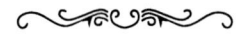

Dear Sister

You've always been so good to me, so happy when we meet,
Although you think I've always walked the wrong side of the street.
There have been times when I have tried to stay close by your side,
But I felt my soul was shackled and my hands and heart were tied.
I couldn't walk the rugged road that led to calvary,
Or pay the price of pleasures lost for Christianity.
But you my loyal sister have stayed both straight and true,
Never quite condemning me no matter what I do.
You always seem to understand that in my heathen way,
I'd never hurt a living soul, although I cannot pray.
So when you get to heaven and your on your saviours knee,
Perhaps once more you'll spare a thought for someone weak like me.
By pleading my unworthy cause, you may decide my fate,
And then maybe the day will come when I'll scrape through the gate.
I'll be a humble servant, I'll pay the price of sin,
I'll freely state that I was wrong if I can just get in.
But if I'm forced to stoke the fire and sing the devils song,
My comfort will be knowing you are where you belong.

Diana Princess of Wales

1961-1997

She was beautiful, compassionate and full of love,
Her innocence was there for all to see.
She left the nation breathless on her royal wedding day,
In her diamonds and her dress of ivory.

A princess who was vulnerable, with tender dreams,
A freshness blowing like a summer breeze.
Fragmented by the protocol in time her heart would break,
Although she tried so very hard to please.

Drowning in bewilderment she made her stand,
And to the world outside she was a star.
She touched the heart of everyone with sympathy and care,
And gave her all to troubles near and far.

What magical enchantment had surrounded her,
What moments of delight she had to give.
Her smile was like a beacon to the lonely and the lost,
And gave the sick the hope and will to live

But now the light has gone, no glimmer left to shine,
Extinguished in a land across the sea.
A nation is in morning for the princess that they loved,
Who will live forever more in history.

Dreams in a Bottle

The man I loved was nothing but a skunk
So I crawled into a bottle and got drunk.

I saw him then through very different eyes
Forgot the meanness and the petty lies.

Thought only of the arms that held me tight
The kisses that could warm my lonely night.

The tender way he called me buttercup
Tis a pity that I had to sober up.

Faces

The anaesthetic didn't numb my brain
I watched the surgeon taking me apart
Inert my body lay as cool as ice
As he skilfully removed my beating heart

I saw his eyes, so cold above the mask
And felt the hands that once caressed my face
Like talons now they carried out the task
Of leaving me behind without a trace

The instruments were placed into his hand
By one, who passed the tools with selfish pride
Yet senselessly he couldn't understand
The many faces standing at his side

Ambitious, an assistant who would learn
To yield the knife with expert skill and ease
And someday he will have to take his turn
Of seeing what this broken body see's

Fairy Tails

I have a great faith in fairy's, have you
And I'm sure that their magical too.
They have sweet fairy rings and gossamer wings
And they make all your wishes come true.

I believe there's a man in the moon
And I'm sure I'll be there with him soon.
In my rocket I'll land and he'll hold out his hand
And together we'll whistle a tune.

Some folk say there's no Santa Claus
But I think they are terrible boars.
He brings gifts on his sleigh which he leaves Christmas day
Then goes back to his homeland and snores.

I believe that the world is alright
And that things don't go bump in the night.
I think everything's good and I know if I could
I would fill every heart with delight.

Father Time

He stood beside the hawthorn bush, the old and withered man,
He saw confusion in my face and took me by the hand.
He led me to the pool of life, and asked me what I saw
Was there something new to me I hadn't seen before.
Of course not was my curt reply, my feet are still quite dry
And all I see is sun and rain, planets, earth and sky.
So that is not enough for you, you hunger to explore
Though life is all around you, you have need for something more.
Well many men have ventured here to search this land of mine
Before you lies the universe and I am father time.
They come here in their search for truth of all eternity
And I have stood and watched them drown in curiosity.
I hesitated on the brink, again he took my hand,
Come my child I'll show the way and help you understand.
Together we explored the paths that all were new to me
Enlightenment, evolution and Christianity.
The powers that open up the mind so many different ways
The theory's of a thousand years, conflicting in the maze.
The minds of many intellects laid out in picture form
But before we reached each ultimate, a new idea was born.
At last I paused exhausted and asked what I should do
My head was in a turmoil, what was false and what was true.
You must decide yourself my child I can't do anymore
But whatever path you walk, you'll never open every door.
Yet you have travelled far today and kept your sanity
So you'll face whatever lies in store with quiet dignity.
But I have travelled further, to the bottom of the pond
And stood there for a million years, yet cannot see beyond.
So go back to the pool of life and tread it without fear
For the answer lies within yourself, the reason we are here.

Free Kuwait

There is no aspect of a war that brings me any joy,
A soldiers grave is not the place to leave a teenage boy.
I can't condone the savagery, the bloodshed or the tears,
And the sound of guns and mortar shell wage torment on my ears.

But, nor can i stand idle when a tyrant rears his head,
And tramples through a nation till it's heart is torn and bled.
I hear the cry for freedom and i cannot turn away,
The sound would echo in my soul and haunt me every day.

I look around at loved ones who may suffer in this war,
Their lives seem far more precious than they ever did before.
I think of words long written," if they all come back but one,
No cause for celebration, he was still some mothers son".

So be it, if my country fights to set a nation free,
I'll wear my cloak of honour and portray my bravery.
But, if my prayers are answered, then the tyrants rule will cease,
And words replace the guns of war, and bring forever peace

Friends

Gifts that grow in nature's earth
Symbolize what friendships worth
Thriving in the sun and rain
Shedding leaves that grow again
Just the way a friend should be
In sadness and prosperity
Stanch, true and always there
Even when the stems are bare
In blossom when the time is right
Although the roots are out of sight
So my darlings I shall know
That as I watch it spread and grow
Until my time on earth is through
I have the gift of friends like you.

1986

Garden of My Life

I sat among beautiful flowers, my future I clearly could see.
To my friends I would always show kindness, and they would return it to me.
I had no desire for riches or fame, contentment was second to none.
My silver I'd find in the light of the moon, my gold in the warmth of the sun.
I would always walk tall with my head held up high,
I would never get angry or wild.
Yes my future shone bright as the stars in the sky, but then I was only a child.

As the years quickly passed I discovered, among flowers there also grew weeds.
Springing to life with abandon, from life's disillusionment seeds.
Though I fought to destroy the intruders, at times it was too hard to tell.
And my ignorance often resulted, in destroying the flowers as well.
So my garden became unattended, my hopes blown away on the breeze.
And the dreams of my childhood were shattered,
Like the crumbling fall of the leaves.

Now I'm much older and wiser, and I've sifted my garden with care.
I have chosen a few of the most precious blooms,
And abandoned the rest in despair.
For I've learnt that the world is not laid at our feet,
That we cannot have acres of land.
Just one single plot is allotted to us, and it has to be carefully planned.
And if you place your trust in one beautiful rose,
And the thorns on the stem become sharp.
You must let the weeds grow till it withers and dies,
Along with the pain in your heart.

Greed

What misery can ere enfold,
As man pursues his quest for gold.
The weary eyes no longer see,
The beauty of a spreading tree.
Then pleading words concealing tears,
Fall only on to empty ears.

Yet still with greed he reaches forth,
To grasp the gifts that gold has bought.
So as he hugs them to his breast,
confused that still he feels unrest.
He hears no tender words that speak,
nor feels soft lips caress his cheek.

But when life's flame is growing dim,
And loneliness sweeps over him.
He doesn't have the price to pay,
For love that's neutered every day.
The profits gained from greed and lust,
Lay worthless in the scattered dust.

Happiness

There's a word that I don't understand mum,
Though the letters I know very well.
I've tried hard to put them together,
But I'm stumped by the word that they spell.
There's an "h" at the very beginning,
That reminds me of hard times we've had.
And the way that the lines crossed your forehead,
When you cried every night over dad.
Next comes an "a" which is clearly,
The anger that came to our door
On the face of the nasty old bailiff
Who said we could sleep on the floor.
And then there are two "ps" that I know mum,
Stands for poverty and being poor
And the hunger I felt in my tummy
When you said, "sorry love there's no more".
Next there's an "I" which I wonder,
Could be me and the line that I chose
And the way that I fought with the children
When they laughed at my old fashioned clothes.
The "n" I am certain means "no love"
For so often you said this to me,
When I asked for a dolls pram for Christmas,
Or a lovely cream bun for my tea.
The "e" is for eyes that are weary
Ah mum, why are yours always sad
Why can't they be eager and shinning
And why can't we have a new dad.
Two "ss" for sordid and squalid
You see I know hard words as well,
I don't think I'm silly or stupid
And I'm sure that I know how to spell.
So I've put all the letters together
But the word I am sure I've not seen
I even know how to pronounce it,
But mum what does happiness mean

I Was There

I was there—I almost saw the light
And faced the great unknown.
The danger zone was imminent, the
Spark of life had flown.

I floated with abandon to the
Dark side of the moon,
And watched the earth below me
As I left it all too soon.

But something seemed to hold me back
I swear I know not why.
A tiny voice within me said
"it wasn't time to die".

God doesn't seem to want me
Well at least until I'm due.
So raise your hands in horror
For I'm back to pester you.

RENE MCDERMOTT 2005

Ireland

Oh, Ireland with your sparkling lakes and fields of emerald green,
Your beauty's incomparable with any thing I've seen.
A tiny piece of heaven you were surely meant to be,
As you nestle like a jewel, surrounded by the sea.

Yet how futile are the bitter wars that rage across your land,
How sad to see a gun replace, friendship in the hand.
Mothers weep as coffins are lowered in the mud,
And wary feet tread pavements stained with young men's blood.

How can a land so beautiful bring happiness and joy,
When lurking on each corner is a weapon to destroy.
Bitterness and hatred command your country fair,
Along with fumes of petrol bombs that now pollute the air.

Your streams are overflowing with tears of grief and pain, while
The shamrock mourns it's magic spell and hangs it's head in shame.
Your people breed confusion, and take their soul to task,
With a face bereft of sunlight, hidden by a mask.

Causes long forgotten are revived within the pack,
While innocents unheeded, are caught inside the trap.
Grant those who have destroyed you, a measure of your worth
Then Ireland may become again, a paradise on earth.

Is Anyone Out There

Give me a man with love in his heart, who can laugh when the chips are down.
Give me a man with a smile on his face that is seldom replaced by a frown.

Give me a man who will service my car and will see that the tyres aren't flat.
Who won't rant and rave if the dinner is burnt or I put my cold feet on his back.

Give me a man who will massage my neck, when I ache from the toils of the day.
Who likes digging gardens and pulling up weeds and chasing my troubles away.

Give me a man who is balding and fat, he needn't be handsome and tall.
As long as a paintbrush fits into his hand and he likes decorating the hall.

Give me a man that I know I can trust for temptation he's bound to resist.
I'd really be happy to give him my heart but I'm sure he doesn't exist.

Jo

You slipped away so silently
And left us all in tears,
But in our hearts your lovely smile
Remains throughout the years.

You were the wind beneath the wings
Of all your loving friends,
Your memory will light the way
To where the rainbow ends.

The suns a little dimmer now
The sky is not so blue,
The stars have hid beneath the clouds
Because we're missing you.

Johnny Palmer

Come on Johnny Palmer we would say,
We want this job your doing done today.
A sense of timeless urgency you bring,
As you smile and say "I'll do it in the spring".

Yet here you are a young man in his prime,
Who, one way or another found the time.
To build a home and serve his family right,
Whilst studying to make the future bright.

So lift your head up high and stand up tall,
You proved your way is right to one and all.
While others boast and talk of doing more,
You honour your commitments, slow but oh so very sure.

Karen

MAY 1969-October1969

Ah Karen you have left me and it's hard to bear the pain.
Of knowing I will never hold you in my arms again.
You were my one and only grandchild and I loved you desperately.
So in your tiny hands you take my heart to heavens nursery.

Last Fight

Like a feather floating on a breeze
Like a sinner praying on her knees
Like a bird that's only just alive
On and on and on, I strive.

Like a leaf that's fallen from the tree
Like a door that doesn't have a key
Like a candle melting neath the flames
Though hope has gone, I struggle just the same.

Perhaps it's time to take a well earned rest
To lose a fight is often for the best.

Leader of the Pack

I loved you Macarooni, you were special from the start
Although you chewed my plants and shoes you crept into my heart.
You led the other dogs astray and taught tricks of yours,
But only you could lead the way and open sliding doors.

I often called you baby and sometimes little friend,
I never knew how sick you were until, the very end.
Your death has left me unprepared, my heart is full of tears
But I thank you for the happiness you brought me through the years.

LOVE MUMMY

Lennon's Peace

A TRIBUTE TO JOHN LENNON

They took a lad from Liverpool and showed him all there is
They raised him up to wealth and fame and said the world was his.
Surrounded by adoring fans he gladly drank the wine
And revelling in glory, he dismissed the hands of time.
But soon his soul grew weary and he reached towards the sky
His heart cried out for something new that money couldn't buy.
Some dreams were found in capsules that nestled in his hand
And he rode the waves of ecstasy society had banned.
No longer could the oak tree, be savoured at a glance
But in the vein within the leaf, he found an olive branch.
He bordered on religion and travelled far and wide
Exploring many cultures to find his soul inside.
Then from his mixed emotions one single dream unfurled
The wish that he desired most was [peace throughout the world].
He gathered his crusaders whilst his music filled the air
And the strains of his imagine was echoed everywhere.
You may say that I'm a dreamer were the haunting words he sung
And he begged us all to join him so the world could be as one.
He inspired his gentle army to conquer fear and strife
Yet cruelly their leader fell as violence took his life.
So lets all strive together, that wars forever cease
And let the years that span henceforth, be known as
Lennon's peace.

Lifeboat

[ode to john]

I know you would much rather live by the sea,
But for twenty eight years you've been stuck here with me. The air is polluted, there's dirt on the street, and you miss the warm breeze and the sand on your feet.

But I'm wild as the water and tough as a rock, and I stand by your side when bad luck comes to knock.
While you are my lifeboat and always will be,
So I'm glad you decided to stay here with me.

Love?

Am I in love? I don't think that can be
Though I didn't eat my breakfast or my tea.
My bra I somehow put on inside out
And my skirt is back to front with out a doubt.
I caught my usual bus, but on reflection
I think I'm going in the wrong direction.

So what is love, I've often heard it said
Its memory loss and going mad instead.
Anticipation fills you every day and
Excitement drives your appetite away.
If someone sold a cure I would buy it
But at least its doing wonders for my diet.

Maureen

Died aged 21

You were so young my tender friend
To slip away so fast
But we can only pray you've found
Your happiness at last.

Medical Intrusion

You came to me with unexpected speed
No time allowed you caught me unprepared.
I always thought my strength would see me through
No fate could leave me trembling or scared.

But silently you crept into my life
You challenged me with mysteries unseen.
My world became confused my mind unsure
But now the time has come to change the scene.

I will not let you win this bitter fight
My destiny will not lie in your hands.
My courage will be solid as a rock
Whilst you will be embedded in the sand.

This warrior was only born to win
And even though your force may strike again.
I'll prove to be superior in strength
And in the end my pride will beat your pain.

Missed

Time is short and life has gone
The coloured rainbow lingers on
The world becomes an empty space
With nothing new to take it's place.

The bygone years are left behind
No stress or trouble cloud my mind
No sound of morning bluebird call
No hurt or teardrop left to fall.

I'll disappear into the sky
A spirit floats it doesn't fly
But one vain thought I can't resist
I like to think that I'll be missed.

Misused Power

In the days of long ago, when bosses had their say
And working men got up at dawn to face a long hard day.
No one turned up late for work, or dared to answer back,
Or fall asleep upon the job, encase they got the sack.

And so we formed a union to stand up for our rights,
And voted in the militants to lead us in our fights.
We campaigned for a shorter week, and rises in our pay,
And extensions on our tea breaks, which we wanted twice a day.

We asked for extra labour force to help relieve the strain,
And more time off to drive our cars, or holiday in Spain.
But then we found with power we could do just what we like.
For if we didn't get our way, we all went out on strike.

Contracts were not honoured, orders fell behind,
And at the gate we picketed until they changed their mind.
And so our lordly bosses, no longer had their way,
With three men doing one mans job, the workers ruled the day.

But fall in productivity and wages soaring high,
Increased the price of everything, so still we couldn't buy.
Our exports were unwelcome, the goods remained unsold,
And cashing in their losses all the firms began to fold.

So god bless all the unions, and what they tried to do,
Tis a pity it was ruined, by the likes of me and you.

Moment in Time

See the snowflakes as they fall, like tattered sheets that once adorned a lover's bed. Watch them float, fragmented in the air, like foolish words, that wisdom would have left unsaid. Far, bereft of unity, with independent solitude, they separate and make their passage one by one. The moment is forever lost, when silent as a whisper in the dawn, they touch the ground and melt beneath the morning sun.

My Best Gal

She makes me feel happy
She makes me feel gay.
So I'll try to explain
Why I love her this way.
She helps me in winter
To keep out the cold.
And her shiny red nose
Is a joy to behold.
She's a dream in the country
A joy in the town.
And I always feel certain
She wont let me down.
We are always together
And travel so far.
That is why I love bb
My little red car.

Nina's Story

I'm glad it's you who rescued me
And fixed my eyes so I could see.
You took me out to walk the street
To keep the claws down on my feet.

Yet still I sometimes shake with fear
But feel much better when your near.
You are the best { my special one }
So thank you dad for all you've done.

Nina

RENE MCDERMOTT 2006

Not Me

I don't want someone who's consumed with passion
And looks at me with ever lustful eyes
Who thinks I should dress up in the evening
With black suspenders pulled across my thighs.

I don't want someone who will buy me diamonds
And drive me round in a great big fancy car
Who wants me to be nice to those in power
But never show my face in a public bar.

I don't want someone who regards me simple
And speaks to me as tho I were a child
Who thinks that my opinions count for nothing
And calls it temper tantrums when I'm wild.

Now the Fighting is Over

Underneath the green hills of the Falkland's
Where the south Atlantic wind blows from the sea,
Our men who fought and died are still together
In a land they travelled many miles to free.

As side by side they faced the bloody battle
What comradeship was surely in each heart,
And silent vows like links in chains of courage
Inspired every man to play his part.

No distance can diminish love and honour
Nor empty arms ache less when grief comes home,
But a mothers tears can fall a little softer
In the knowledge that her son is not alone.

They will not be forgotten in the morrow
Although they lie so many miles away,
For Jesus Christ was buried on a hillside
Yet his courage is remembered to this day.

Playing the Double

You knew the cost, the price was high, the situation do or die.
But, still you choose to place your bet, a double scoop you hoped to get.
On tenterhooks you played along, regardless of the right or wrong.
No sad remorse for mortal sin, just take a chance and hope to win

Oh, how ambitious you became, as cheating entered in the game.
Your hand was played with all the gall, of one who knows he's pledged his all.
Well, you lost the dream you lusted for, you lost your pride and what is more.
You lost your bet, and at the end, you even lost your dearest friend.

Poor

I read the poem that you sent, which made me feel quite discontent
Why should I always work and slave, until I'm carried to my grave.
Too long I've been collecting fares and running up and down the stairs,
Helping old dears with their shopping, shouting hold tight as were stopping.
Folding pushchairs holding babies, squeezing past the fat old ladies,
So to work I went next day, determined not to earn my pay.
Upon the bus I chose a seat and claimed another for my feet
And when the public clambered on, I just laid back and sang a song.
My driver shouted "where's the bell" but I replied "ah go to hell"
I don't care if were here all day, cause on my arse I'm going to stay.
And if they want to pay their fares, they'll have to leave it on the stairs
Just then it seemed from out the blue, a big inspector came in view.
What's this he cried you can't sit down and leave your driver running round
Not knowing when to stop and start, you'll give him wind and make him fart.
But I just cocked my legs up high I turned to him and with a sigh said
"I'd rather be at home, than work my fingers to the bone".
"ah well" he said, "in that case dear we certainly don't want you here"
And then without a lot of fuss, he promptly threw me off the bus.
So now I've taken your advise and stayed at home which is quite nice
I'm sure I'll live to ninety four, the trouble is I'm bloody poor.

Questions

No little chap, I do not know, exactly how the flowers grow,
Or why the storm roars overhead when you are safely tucked in bed.
I just can't think why it should be, the sun shines when you have your tea,
Or why it always starts to rain when you go out to play again.

No my boy I'm not to sure, why cats miaow and lions roar,
Or why a zebras black and white and owls make noises in the night.
Why houses grow on backs of snails and foxes all have bushy tails,
Or rabbits live inside a hutch, why do you have to know so much ?

And no my son I don't know why, mummy left and made us cry,
But what you're saying isn't true, she didn't just stop loving you.
So close your eyes and go to sleep, don't brush your hand across my cheek,
Of course it's not a silly tear, it's just a bit too hot in here.

Ah, now you're sleeping son of mine, so that's the end of question time,
I slowly creep towards the door, then turn back to your bed once more.
I bet you think your dads a fool, who didn't learn a thing at school,
Believe me son, I wish I knew, but I need answers just like you.

Ride the Rainbow

Where will you be when they push the button,
And blow this world of ours to kingdom come.
Will they catch you riding on a rainbow,
Or basking in the rays of golden sun.

Will your eyes be shining with excitement,
Your heart be filled with happiness and joy.
Or will you still be fighting losing battles,
As the politicians detonate their toy.

There may not be a future for our children,
The bomb has been designed sadistically.
And lunatics will use their evil power,
Not caring what it does to you and me.

But we cannot fight their weapons with our feelings
Yet if we wear our badge of courage well.
We will ride so high above them on our rainbow,
We can watch them blow each other in to hell.

Riding High

The Air balloon was on the ground and Sidney stepped inside,
It was his life ambition to go up for a ride.

The crowd were all excited, the weather was just right
When Sidney said, "excuse me please, I've wet myself with fright"

Well, they let him change his trousers, and he sighed with great relief,
Then placed inside his navel hole, a lucky clover leaf

With baited breath he waited, to be raised up in the air,
The helium was set in force, a brighten golden glare

The gas was rising upwards, the balloon was big and round
But though they turned the pressure up it would not leave the ground

The organiser stepped aboard and cried "what's this down here"
"No wonder it won't take the weight with twenty crates of beer"

"Well", said Sid "what's wrong with that, you surely do not think,
I'm floating up in the clouds, without a bloomin drink"

So they handed him a bottle of good old navy rum
And threw the beer crates overboard, the problem overcome

Then as it slowly left the ground, they saw old Sidney grin
As from his pocket he produced, a flagon filled with Gin

"I'd rather have my beer" he said, "but Gin and Rum will do
I'm not keen on either, so ill have to mix the two

well the mixture he concocted was so potent and so rare
That the fumes went rising upwards, and polluted all the air

Instead off floating slowly the balloon began to race
It shot across the Irish Sea at quiet a rapid pace

Then when it reached Killarney, the fumes began to die
And all the Irish paddy's watched it come down form the sky

They thought it was a space ship from Jupiter or mars
And took our Sidney on a trip to all the pubs and bars

You can't go back they said to Sid, but he just stood and grinned
Then jumped into his air balloon and started passing wind

It shot off like a rocket beyond the speed of sound
Across the wide Atlantic where America is found

And when it got to Washington said Regan like as not
I sent the thing up there myself oh boy I just forgot

Sid felt himself descending but before he got too far
He raised a second wind to dodge that old B movie star

The gases sent him soaring high, the speed was quite horrific
Before old Sid could blink an eye, he'd crossed the north pacific

Excitement filled the Kremlin as they gazed up at the sky
Excuse Mr Gorbachev I think we have a spy

The Russian leader shook with rage and cried I need a catcher
To stop that man reporting back to crafty Mrs Thatcher

He sent his first class pilots up and bring him down they did
What do you want said Gorbachev a vodka please said Sid

The empty bottles piled up high, the Russians slapped his thigh
Now come on Sid I want to know your secret of the sky

Ah well said Sid I must admit I had some trouble starting,
But after that the secret is I just excel at farting

The celebrations on red square, went on all day and night
Then all the Russians bottled wind for Sidney's homeward flight

Our differences with Russia, have been reduced to zero
Gorbachev loves Thatcher cos Sid is now his hero

So peace now reins throughout the world, at least it will do soon
When Sid returns to England's shores inside his big balloon

Still Waiting

I remember very well, the year we had the heat wave spell,
We laughed and played upon the sand, you kissed my cheek and held my hand.
In cotton top and flowered skirt, we skipped barefoot on woodland dirt,
And fearing I would come to harm, you caught me safely on your arm.
Rabbits played among the dunes, we danced to soft romantic tunes,
And when you left to go away, you promised you'd come back one day.
Well, time has gone and years have flown, and still I sit here all alone,
Days are cold and nights are bleak, a bottle warms my frozen feet.
The flowered skirt and cotton top, are hanging in the Oxfam shop,
And often when I try to speak, a salty tear runs down my cheek.
Yet, in my dreams I call your name, and you are at my side again,
I gaze into your soulful eyes, and bash you up for telling lies.

Streetwalker

Night birds rising from the shadows walk the streets of shame
High heeled sandals clicking softly in the winter rain.
Pausing neath the neon lighting watching cars appear
Provocatively confident, yet hiding inward fear.

Faces blurred by glaring headlights, speed on through the night
Hurry home to warm embraces day is done delight.
Honking horns from teenage morons driving reckless round the town
Obscene words assault the eardrums as they wind the windows down.

Kerbstone crawlers drawing near door swings open gradually
Yellow teeth are showing clearer as he ventures, what's your fee.
Swift exchange of paper money grubby fingers on the thigh
Putrid breath and perspiration, at least inside the car it's dry.

Night time breaks into the morning stagger home on weary feet
Find the baby sitter dozing little children fast asleep.
Lots of bread for hungry tummy's need for crumpled notes to pay
First remove unloving hand marks scrub the sordid night away.

Tell Me About the War Nan

Tell me about the war Nan,
Who was it started the fight.
What do they mean by the "blackout",
And how did they see without light.

Why was the food all on ration?
And why did the shopkeeper say
That you couldn't have sweeties or chocolate
Even though you had money to pay.

Why did the Germans drop bombs "Nan"
That hurt little children like me,
And when people slept in the shelter
Did they take down a big flask of tea.

Who was the man they called "Winnie",
And why did they make him a star,
Did he have muscles like "Popeye?"
Or like superman with a cigar.

Why did the men go to war Nan
Leaving women and children alone,
And did mummy's cry in their tea cups
For the ones who would never come home.

I know that the fighting is over
And it happened a long time ago
But tell me about the war Nan,
Cos I think it's important to know.

That Girl

Throw that big stone in the river Jimmy, see how the ripples swirl
Lets just pretend that were here on our own and not with that silly girl.
Its horrible having her hanging around, but mum said I must be nice
She lived in a place on the edge of the moor, which we visited once or twice.
But last week her cottage burnt to the ground and they've taken her mother away,
They say she'll be gone for a long long time, so we had to invite her to stay.
But she screams when I dangle a worm in her face or I tug on her pigtails at school
And she doesn't like tadpoles, beetles or frogs and she's hopeless at kicking a ball.

Oh, look at that wood that is floating along, what a wonderful raft it could be
Lets go and get it and pull it ashore and we'll share it between you and me.
Hey watch it I think there's a dip over there oh crikey your floundering Jim
I cannot do more than to stretch out my hand for I never did learn to swim.
As I helplessly stand here with tears in my eyes, that girl swiftly passes me by,
With her hand neath your chin she heads back for the shore and I'm trying my best not to cry.
For I know that she's hopeless at kicking a ball and she washes at least twice a day
But I wouldn't have you as my friend anymore, if she hadn't been with us today.

That Handbag

I walked into the Oxfam shop
I'd been there once before
Disposing of some goods
I had no use for anymore.

As I looked around me
A handbag caught my eye
It brought back many memories
And made me want to cry.

The leather bore the signs of age
The clasp had lost its shine
But many precious gifts had
Been inside that bag of mine.

Rattles that had lost their charm
Sweets in little tins
Hair grips that had fallen out
And even nappy pins.

Booties kicked from tiny feet
Hankies trimmed with lace
A cloth for sticky fingers
That I carried just in case.

The Babes of Tribulation

On the 27th of January 1991, everyman BBC 1 screened a programme
Concerning the children being shot and mutilated by the police in Guatemala.
On the 28th of January 1991, ITV's world in action, showed the same thing
occurring in Rio de Janeiro, this time by a group of vigilantes.

There are children in the streets of Guatemala,
But there isn't any laughter in their eyes.
Their world consists of poverty and hunger,
And survival is the mainspring of their lives.

They fear the one's who should be their protectors,
Narcotics help to take away the pain.
And often broken bodies line the pavements,
Too badly hurt to ever rise again.

It's much the same in Rio de Janeiro,
Where vigilantes hunt the children down.
Like animals they hide in darkened doorways,
As night casts evil shadows on the town.

I look upon the faces of these children,
Such tiny tragic lives bereft of treats.
But why has god decided to desert them,
And left the ghost of death, upon the streets.

I know my faith has often been in question,
I've never been committed to the truth.
I've always needed something more to guide me,
A vision or a sign, to give me proof.

But as I watch the faces of the children,
So wantonly abandoned in this way.
I find my faith is clouded with confusion,
And my doubts grow even stronger every day.

The Blackberry Man

Have you seen the blackberry man
He comes round at three.
He picks them from down yonder hedge
And brings them home to me.

He sits down in the corner
While I bake a golden pie.
His fingers stained all black and blue
A twinkle in his eye.

We sit and talk of all the fun
We had so long ago.
Of how we lived from off the land
And kept warm in the snow.

Then for a fleeting moment
I am taken back in time.
I wonder what I am doing
In this comfy home of mine.

I once ran barefoot round a field
A child of seventeen.
Waiting for the lover
Who would soon fulfil my dreams.

Well he courted me with diamonds
He bought me with his gold.
He showered me with tempting gifts
Till I was bought and sold.

So I forfeited my freedom
And I never see the stars.
The gadgets and the microwave
Just serve as prison bars.

I'm like a bird within a cage
Who now and then gets free.
That's when my dad the blackberry man
Comes round to have his tea.

The Bright Tomorrow

A war is coming so they say
Will we face another day
Or will we all get blown away
Tomorrow.

Should we all abandon hope
Care not that we cannot cope
Sever faith and cut the rope
Tomorrow.

Face the future days ahead
Feeling low and filled with dread
Or plan our future lives instead
Tomorrow.

Well i for one will stand and fight
Embrace the hours day and night
Convinced that things will be alright
Tomorrow.

The Choice

The devil sang his song to me I heard it loud and clear,
He said that if I follow him I'd never have to fear.
He'd help me to compose my lies and trample on my friends,
And disregard my conscience to ensure my wicked ends.

He said that if I enjoyed myself I wouldn't have a care,
I'd feel no pain or sympathy for others in despair.
There wouldn't be a spark of love to ache within my heart,
And with my selfish greedy gains I'd never have to part.

The angles sang a different song that softly begged me stay,
I had to listen carefully to what they had to say,
No gifts of gold were offered no path bereft of strife,
And pain might be the price I pay for love within my life.

But I'd glow with satisfaction from doing what was right,
I'd bask within the sunshine sleep contented through the night.
And loving hands of friendship would guide me all day long,
So casting out the devil I have chose the angles song.

The Craftsman

I watch as you work with meticulous care,
On the model you hold in your hand.
A few bits of plastic and a small pot of paint,
Taking form of a boat on a stand.
When a man carves a flute from a raw piece of wood,
Or grown flowers from working the earth.
He's creating a beauty from nothing at all,
Which is proving just what he is worth.
But to put into practice that patience and care,
With the feelings of those all around you.
Is creating a masterpiece in your own soul,
And love is the frame that surrounds you.

The Fighter

Along the rugged road of life she trod,
Determined to stay in the sight of god.

But as the road began to turn and bend,
She chose the demon drink as her best friend.

The hands that longed to help were pushed aside,
As the ugly head reared upwards of false pride.

And loved ones hearts were crushed like empty shells,
As she struggled onwards in her private hell.

But then one day she added up the score,
As the gutter lay there like an open sore.

Then she lifted up her head and faced the sky,
Crying "lord I promise nothing, but I'll try".

The Fox and the Clown

There once was a clown with a smile on his face,
For he had nothing else to commend him.
No beauty or assets or glamorous looks,
But the lack of them didn't offend him.

He took all the troubles that life sent his way,
And pushed them aside with distraction.
For by playing the fool, he could make people laugh,
And that gave him great satisfaction.

Then one day the crafty old fox came along,
Who had spent all his life being subtle.
He'd plundered and cheated wherever he went,
Then when things got too hot he would scuttle.

He'd venture to pastures more tempting and green,
Where the people would be unsuspecting.
Then he'd lay in his lair until someone arrived,
Who was foolish enough to respect him.

And so came the day when the fox met the clown,
And he weedled his way to affection.
The clowns faithful friends slowly faded away,
As the fox begged for all his attention.

But, when he was sure he had captured his heart,
He went back to fulfilling his needs.
And those who could see without love in their eyes,
Told the clown of his treacherous deeds.

He wouldn't believe all the story's they told,
Just thought they were being unfair.
But as time went by and the truth came to light,
His heart almost broke with despair.

The smile slowly faded, he died by degrees,
Had no strength left to fight the corrupt
And the fox showed no pity, or even remorse,
But just greedily gobbled him up.

The Gap

A girl born in a London street
A country boy with itchy feet
Intention was you wouldn't meet
At all

And yet despite the miles and years
You found each others smiles and tears
And shared hopes, dreams and fears
What gall

Whatever kept you by my side
Your differences were vast and wide
Destroying faith and causing pride
To fall

Yet still you chose to carry on
It seemed the ties were much too strong
You faced, whenever things went wrong
A wall

I'm a sharer you're a taker
When at last we meet our maker
Spruced up by the undertaker
He will say

When I put you two on earth
Organized and planned your birth
I thought you both would make it worth
The stay

Instead of that it seems to me
You brought each other misery
So don't expect much sympathy
Today

For back when I created you
With many years between the two
I never thought you'd misconstrue
The way

The Gold Seeker

I walked among the leafy trees
Wellie boots up to my knees.
Big straw hat as my protector
And in my hand a metal detector.
Buzz, buzz, buzz it buzzed around
There must be something in the ground.
Would I now enjoy my leisure
Living it up on buried treasure.
Quickly I groped on the ground
But silver paper was all I found.

So I trundled home again
My search for gold had been in vain.
My dreams of being a millionaire
Had burst like bubbles in the air.
But when I reached my humble place
Saw my loved ones shining face.
Smelt the dinner slowly cooking
Found my slippers without looking.
I sank back happy in the chair
And knew I was a millionaire.

The Happy Ending

I'm not a tree, I will not be, forever, I'm just a twig, not very big, however. I wonder why, if I should die, tomorrow, there's sure to be, some misery and sorrow. For, I, have seen the warm sunbeam, in splendour and watched the leaf that falls in sweet September. My life was fine, I had no time for grieving, but weary be the part of me that's leaving. So, prune the tree and think of me hereafter, as redesigned to leave behind, the laughter.

The Juvinile Delinquent

The girl was waiting in the dock accused of petty crime,
Her mother sat in anguish remembering the time.
When as a tiny baby by her cradle she had prayed,
Oh god don't let my darling die please let her life be saved.
But was this what I prayed for that one day she should be,
A juvenile delinquent, and bring disgrace to me.
Was it that I spoilt her and let her have her way,
Or was it the love I gave that has brought her here today.

The trial was nearly over the verdict had been cast,
The daughter looked around and met her mother's eyes at last.
And when she saw the work worn face, the bitter unshed tears,
She thought oh god I've hurt her oh, please turn back the years.
But no, that never can be done so I can only pray,
That he who choose to save my life will save my soul today.
Once more she gazed at that dear face so lined and worn with care,
And knew her mother understood and saw forgiveness there.

The Kiss

Ah, yes I remember it well mum,
The day that our dad went away.
You gathered us children together,
And told us to go out and play.

You said when you finished your breakfast,
You would both come and join in our game.
Then we'd all catch a bus to the station,
Where daddy would get on a train.

Well, we all had a peep through the window,
There was Carrie and Bobby, and me.
And though we were watching you closely,
It was clear that you just didn't see.

For, as you reached out for the teapot,
Majestically poised on the stand.
Daddy caught hold of your fingers,
And planted a kiss on your hand.

Then we all made our way to the station.
And we ardently waved him goodbye.
In his uniform he looked so handsome,
That I thought you were silly to cry.

Well, he never came back from the war mum,
And I never did quite understand.
But whenever you reach for the teapot,
I can still see his kiss on your hand

The Last Goodbye

Take me up the wooden hill to bed mum
I'm tired and I need to get some rest.
Then tuck me in and sing me little songs mum
You know the ones I like the very best.

I heard the doctor say I'm getting weaker
And saw the tearstains on your lovely face.
So I know it wont be long before I leave mum
To join the angels in their special place.

I don't mind if you tell me little fibs mum
Pretending that tomorrow will be fine.
For I know that your silent prayers have always been mum
That god would take your life instead of mine.

So if the angels come before the morning
And take me to this heaven up above.
Remember that I sleep in sweet contentment
For you gave the greatest gift—a mothers love.

The Legacy

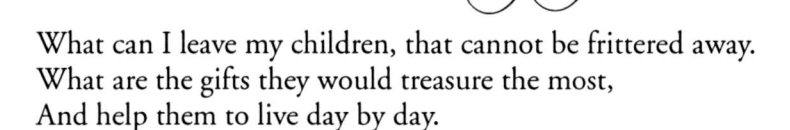

What can I leave my children, that cannot be frittered away.
What are the gifts they would treasure the most,
And help them to live day by day.

I will get me a box made of stardust, that is sure to reflect in their eyes
And I'll pack it with straw stripped from beautiful dreams,
And sprinkle a few gentle sighs

And under the straw there will nestle, the gifts I have chosen with care
Like tenderness, love and compassion, and the grace to be honest and fair

I will pop in a package of kindness and another of light-hearted fun
And I'll drop in a few pearls of wisdom, so they know how to please everyone.

Then I'll tie up the parcels with courage. to ensure that they don't fall apart
And I'll leave them a bonus of wishes come true, for the place that they held in my heart,

The Miner

Carry me up to the top Sam
Where the clouds float along in the sky
Just let me feel the cool breeze on my face
For a moment before I die.

I spent most of my life in the pit Sam
Was no more than a lad at the start
But the coal dust that covers my lungs and my skin
I have never let blacken my heart.

I was never a one to complain Sam
That the darkness commanded my life
My reward for the years in the bowels of the earth
Was the care of my kids and my wife.

So carry me up to the top Sam
Let me take one more look at the sky
And let the green grass be the last thing I feel
In the moment before I die.

The Phoenix

I watched as you stumbled and forge your dignity
As you crawled into a bottle to escape reality.
I wept to think so fine a mind, so beautiful a soul
Could curtsy to destruction and let life take its toll.
I heard the strangled anguished cries that hunted you so long
Whilst demons fought their mindless war and sang the devils song.
What nights were lost in stupor as you groped on through the haze
What misery encountered as you forfeited your days.
No hands could sooth the troubled mind or lead the way ahead
Nor friendships suit of armour protect the conscious dread.
But inner strength was immanent you fought with all your might
You took your courage in both hands and won a gallant fight.
How proud I am to call you friend to watch you prove your worth
To see you walk with head held high and compliment the earth.
With the courage of the phoenix that refused to burn and die
You rose up from the ashes and soared into the sky

The Sea

I looked at the sea through the eyes of a child
And it sparkled all silver and blue.
The waves were like cornets of candy floss
And it showed a magnificent view.
I rode on the surf that was gentle and warm
As the fishes went swimming by.
And the joy of that wonderful watery scene
Took my breath—that I cannot deny.

I looked at the sea through the eyes of a man
But strangely the beauty was dead.
The cruel waves lashed and beat on the shore
As the stormy clouds gathered ahead.
Like matchsticks the debris of ships bobbled along
And a fisherman's hat floated by.
And for all the souls lost in that wild cruel sea
I was sad—that I cannot deny.

How sad are the changes from childhood to man
How different the view that we see.
The shimmering fish that we once called friends
Are not as we thought them to be.
The waves we believed were a sight to behold
Can destroy as the sea becomes wild.
So because I am captured by all it involves
I will watch it through the eyes of a child.

The Seafarer

Just an old sailor people may say
Just an old man of the sea.
Living the last precious years of his life
In acceptance of what was to be.

Carrying on in his own quiet way
With a dignity second to none.
Preparing the future for those whom he loved
By leaving no problem undone.

Tho weary his body and tired his mind
He captained life's ship till the end.
Relating his tales of the places he'd been
When he greeted each day as a friend.

Yes just an old sailor people may say
Who has finally drifted ashore.
But to those who remember the love in his heart
He will always be very much more.

The Silent Homecoming

Seventeen British hero's, are flying home today,
While loved ones in their sorrow stand and wait.
The greeting will be silent as their coffin's leave the plane,
For they left their lives behind them in Kuwait.

In memory they will always be forever young and strong,
Prepared to give their all for victory.
They will not know the sorrow or the pain of growing old,
Or face the years that bring uncertainty.

But, nor will they feel comfort in a woman's loving arms,
Or see the sunshine in a baby's smile.
The desert sands have robbed them of the pleasures yet to come,
And the many things that make our lives worthwhile.

So, let us all remember for as long as we shall live,
The sacrifice that we today have seen.
And send a kiss to heaven on a gentle cloud of love,
For the courage of the silent seventeen.

The Soul Searcher

You who believe there are wonders beyond
That this life is a moment in time.
May I just for a moment, look into your soul
To enrich this complacence of mine.
What can it be that you wish to achieve,
That you cannot clasp tight in your hand.
Is there a beauty more pleasing to see
Than the sea washing over the sand.

Do you believe there are pleasures more rare
Than when lovers let passions run wild.
Is there more tenderness somewhere out there
Than a mother can feel for her child.
And if there is joy, such as we've never known
And the pleasures are greater by far.
Then will we find sorrow that's harder to bear
Will the hurt leave a much deeper scar.

For if we feel love, we must surely feel pain
Or else we feel nothing at all.
When the tree is cut down and the roots spread
Again, will it grow to be fruitful and tall.
Or will it be barren without any leaves
For fear that in time they'll decay.
If this is the picture I see in your soul,
I will cherish my dreams of today.

The Spell

The "white witch "came and cast her spell,
I must admit she done it well
His soul is in eternal hell,
So sad.

He gained respect before she came,
But "psycho's slave "is now his name,
His friends all say he's not to blame
She's bad.

Yet still they thought he'd never be
A victim of her sorcery,
She was as everyone could see
Quite mad.

I know he put up quite a fight,
To keep his head and do what's right,
But witches cling and hold on tight
Poor lad.

With innocence she chose to speak
And as her hair brushed past his cheek,
He couldn't see the evil streak
She had.

Perhaps I should have played my part
And fought to mend his broken heart,
But she decided from the start
To maim.

For underneath that vacant face
There lies a soul that's fell from grace,
A "hag "that hides without a trace
Of shame.

She tried destroying me as well
For on his tongue she placed a spell,
That spat out words from darkest hell
They came.

Too bad, the things she planned so long
Have fizzled out and gone so wrong,
She met her match my mind is strong
And sane.

But, he poor man cannot escape
She wraps him in her witch's cape
And keeps him in a constant state,
Of pain.

The Wall

Gingerly I stepped out on the open road
And walked with hesitation day by day.
I stumbled very often, for a year or two
For many parts were sand instead of clay.

But just the same, I struggled on determinedly
Intending to stay with it to the end.
Yet many times I faltered with uncertainty
As I fought my way around every turn and bend.

Then gradually the road became a leafy lane
The ground was soft the air was filled with song.
I made my way, complacent in security
As my feet took wings and carried me along.

But now, I face a wall, a wall of discontent
I cannot break it down or pass it by.
This road is at an end, there's nowhere left to go
The wall is much too strong and far too high.

So once again I wander in the wilderness
Unsure of what direction I should choose.
I gave my all regardless of the consequence
And now I find I've nothing left to loose.

So maybe I should rest beneath a shady tree
And stay until the leaves begin to fall.
Yet somehow I'm convinced I'll come alive again
And find a road, a road without a wall.

This Unholy War

It's started now, the world has gone to war,
Sophisticated weapons fill the sky.
The time for turning back is here no more,
And brave men must prepare to fight and die.

We see the tyrant on his knees in prayer,
But we pray too, and somehow god must choose.
It seems that he is needed everywhere,
But one side has to win, and one must loose.

How can the great almighty take the strain,
So many pledge their faith to him in prayer.
While wives and mothers make their plea in vain,
He cannot show his mercy everywhere.

What right have we to call on him this way,
And say that when we fight he's at our side.
He did not make the weapons that will slay,
The enemy that we must override.

We fight to rid injustice in the land,
And for this cause we keep our conscience clear.
We should not drag his name through blood and sand,
To help us strike our enemy with fear.

For god is not an instrument of war,
So let him rest in heaven up above.
And when our broken bodies fight no more,
Tis then, we will remember, "God is love".

Thomas And Jason, 1998

Brothers in arms I hear you say
Are they a pop group of today?
Are they a squad of military men?
Or flower pot people like Bill and Ben

No, they are sons of John and Leanne
The product of love tween woman and man.
Surrounded by love they will never be sad
           Safe in the arms of their mummy and dad.

Time {or The Lack of It}

Time seems short now I've turned fifty
Feet and fingers aren't so nifty
Days and hours hurry past
Know just what I want at last
Time to reap and time to sow
Time to watch my garden grow
Show my love to faithful friends
Find out where the rainbow ends
Discover nature when and why
How do insects multiply
Paint a picture write a book
Count the ripples in a brook
Time to watch the shifting sand
Catch a moonbeam in my hand
See the sights I missed before
Hid behind conventions door
Climb the hills and roam the dales
Talk to frogs and worms and snails
Time to try to understand
Why there's hatred in the land
All these things I know I'll do
If I've time to see them through
One thing is I know for sure
I wish I'd done it all before.

Time {The Healer}

I stood among the monuments of long ago
And heard the cries, from ere a thousand years.
The clouds absorbed the sorrows that hung over me
And rivers ran a race, of lonely tears.
I felt the heartache all around engulfing me
My body pained with all, the untold grief.
A plaintive cry was in the crickets hollow call
And lines of sorrow, lay on every leaf.
I knew that if I stood and waited patiently
That time would pass and sorrow disappear.
One day I'd throw aside this cloak of misery
Or drown within the essence of a tear.
Then suddenly the sun began to shine again
It's golden crystals beaming on my face.
I felt my body warm with joy and ecstasy
Twas then that I rejoined the human race.

To Each His Own

I know the world can end without a warning
And leave behind a sinner such as me.
I know that I should be prepared to suffer
As Jesus did that day on Calvary.

For me, there's no excuse or special reason
The gospel has been preached both loud and clear.
So if my life is not in serving Jesus
It simply that I've chosen not to hear.

But, what about the man who worships Buddha
Or the Hindu who believes his faith is true.
Will they all be left to Armageddon
Condemned because they held at a different view.

And, sadly there are children in the ghettos
Where trickery is needed to survive.
To honour and obey the ten commandments
Would sacrifice their chance to stay alive.

So, I cannot wear the uniform of Jesus
Or fight the war that Christians learn from birth.
For my wish is not to be a star in heaven
But to practice peace and love while here on earth.

Tomorrow is Another Day

Will you, wont you, what's your game,
Do you, don't you, know my name.
Have you, did you, wink at me,
Can I, is it, love I see.

Tell me, show me, what you mean,
Are things always what they seem.
First you, then you, lead me on,
Are you here or have you gone.

What if, and if, I'm confused,
Was I loved or was I used.
Should you, would you, give me proof,
Tell me lies or tell the truth.

So what, know what, I don't care,
Let this be a night to share.
Will you, wont you, wish to stay,
Tomorrow beckons come what may.

Confused, you will be !!

Trains

Watch the train that's leaving
Lovers holding hands
Some will part for ever
To far off distant lands.

Quiet tears are falling
Sadness fills the air
Parting is such sweet sorrow
Far beyond compare.

See the train arriving
Watch the faces glow
People waving madly
Calling out hello.

Lots of hugs and kisses
Laughter fills the air
The atmosphere electric
Way beyond compare.

What Have I Done

What have I done to upset you it really must have hurt, you put
Your red trews in the washing machine and ruined my nice white shirt.

I was looking forward to dinner, a steak and kidney pie
But the meat turned out to be gristle and the pastry was cold and dry.

Then when I looked round for my slippers on their place beside the hearth,
You said they were outside drying as you'd dropped them in the bath.

And I know that I left my baccy, on the table by the door
But now the tin has been opened and my baccy's all over the floor.

So why am I sat with my boots on and why is your face so hard,
Ah yes, but of course I remember, I've forgotten your birthday card.

Will I Make the Grade

Will there be an inquest as I stand at heavens gate,
Will my worldly acts and deeds decide upon my fate.
How will I excuse myself, for stepping out of line,
Indulged in idle boredom and wasting precious time.

Will I be forgiven for speaking hasty words,
Or throwing crusts of bread away that could have fed the birds.
Will I be confronted with a loved ones sorry plight,
Deprived of any comfort, by the note I didn't write.

Will my sins be magnified, or lightly brushed aside,
Condemned for all my failures, or praised because I tried.
I hope st peter smiles at me and takes me by the hand,
And leads me through the golden gates, into the promised land.

Willing to Learn

Teach me lord to listen well, and not jump to conclusions,
Teach me how to give advise, without direct intrusion.
Teach me to appreciate the outstretched helping hand,
And never to condemn the times they fail to understand.

Teach me how to find the words to comfort those in need,
And never to expect reward for every kindly deed.
Teach me how to face the years, and not regret my youth,
But, most of all, pray teach me lord, to recognise the truth.

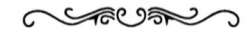

Would I

To see all the world through the eyes of trust
To listen with hearing of truth,
To believe all the fighting was only a game
See hands clasped together in proof.

To know there's no hunger, no cross brought to bear
On a man for his colour or creed,
Abolish emotions designed to destroy
Like jealousy, anger and greed.

To watch the spring flowers burst through the earth
Though the frost lays it's carpet of white,
To feel the warm sun that can brighten the day
Continue to shine in the night.

But would I with wonder regard the sweet rose
Blossom forth where the weeds had been planted,
Or would I sit back with an air of distain
And be taking the hole scene for granted.

Yobs

Why don't you turn around old man, you must know we are here,
We watched you amble in the pub, to buy a pint of beer.
We stared at your old fashioned clothes that really made us laugh,
And where did you get that kipper tie and bright red woolly scarf.

You know old man, your ugly, and old enough to die,
Your hands are bent and crippled and your skin is cracked and dry.
Why don't you turn and argue, or even blow your top,
Or maybe you could whine a bit and beg us please to stop.

That's it old man, you've turned around, but what's this that we hear,
You're telling us how nice we look in all our fancy gear.
And how we make it all worthwhile for fighting two world wars,
But you cannot stay and gossip cause your hearing aids indoors.

Its no use saying sorry, you wouldn't understand,
Instead we pat you on the back and shake your crippled hand.
You never heard the thoughtless words that would have caused you pain,
But you wont be disillusioned should we ever meet again.

You and Me

Remember how things used to be
We had such fun did you and me.
The car free roads on which we played
And raffled jars of marmalade.

The war was on but did we care
Th'o bombs were dropping everywhere.
We laughed and played and put on shows
In fancy dress and satin bows.

Then off we'd trot to Uxbridge fair
And chat the boys that gathered there.
We so indulged the latest craze
Those happy sunny childhood days.

Later on as years went by
We both got jobs did you and I.
And Sunday mornings without shame
We'd both go off to petticoat lane.

There we'd search until we found
Some earrings costing half a crown.
Then all dressed up from toes to top
We danced all night at the shilling hop.

Now sixty plus eight years more
With angels knocking at the door.
There's one thing that is clear to see
I've still got you and you've got me.

Snippets

Snippets 1

I saw the sun between the trees,
I felt the soft warm summer breeze.

I touch the leaves all moist with dew,
But who the flipping heck are you.

You looked into my starry eyes,
And promised not to tell me lies.

I fell in love with an ostrich
I fed him on stilton cheese
He would have liked gorgonzola
But he never once learned to say please.

I wandered away in my dreams last night
To the place where the odd socks go.
Whirling and twirling they danced around
As the wind made an effort to blow.

I saw some old friends as I wandered around
A sock with a moon and a star.
Its partner was left in the washing machine
And I used it to polish the car.

There was one that I wore when I slept in a tent
And the weather was freezing and damp.
I kept my socks on but when morning arrived
The left one had flown from the camp.

Then old stripes appeared
I remembered it well.
They were long almost up to my knees
But the basket of laundry just gobbled it up.

Snippets 2

Cold, cold custard pink striped mustard
Salt and pepper for your tea.
Gooseberry jam and a half cooked ham
That's a lot for you and me.

Those nasty little calories
Jumped in my apple pie.
They spread their horrid
Balls of fat along my sylph like thigh.

My greasy roast potatoes
Should have given them the slip.
But still the buggers hopped
Inside and settled on my hip.

Nostalgia is the last refuge of the moron.

Reach for the moonbeams in the sky
Gather them in your hand.
Fill every moment of every day
With the magic of wonderland.
Be not afraid of the tender shoots
That symbol the signs of change.

Deer have this ability, when their
Hopelessly trapped. Just to die.
Their heart explodes or something.

These tumbling pigs will make you smile, whenever you are blue.
The bird that nestles in the tree will calm and comfort you.
The soft elusive butterfly will thrill you with its beauty.
But shield your eyes from the jumping frog, unless you're feeling fruity.

Snippets 3

I will not die in the springtime
When the magnolia trees in bloom.
Or the golden rays of the summer sun
Fill the corners of my room.
I will wait till the winds of winter
Freeze the frost upon the ground.

Christmas time is here again
Take an aspirin for the pain
Children want expensive gifts
Designer labels on their lists
They look at you like you're insane
You bought the wrong computer game
We eat too much it's not a joke
End up fat, worn out and broke.

I peeped in the window to where you were stood
I would have embraced you if only I could
But someone had entered and stood by your side
And the love that you showed them could not be denied
Well I stood in the rain and my heart broke in two
I thought it was me that was special to you.

Snippets 4

Safe haven

Out of the sunlight far from the springtime flowering,
Into the jaws of monsters dark and devouring.
Far from the tender arms that brought me redemption
Into a lonely world of utter rejection.

How could a word unspoken fill me with sorrow?
Why must I face the pain that comes with tomorrow?
Let me sleep on and in my slumbered vacation
Enter the warm embrace that grants me salvation.

Can you bring me consolation
Can you take away the pain
Can you mend a shattered heart
And help me come alive again.

Can you stop my hands from shaking
Can you dry my tear filled eyes
Can you make me wake with wonder
As the sun begins to rise.

Snippets 5

Oh promise me that someday when my soul has gone to rest
And the memories of my smile are growing dim.

That sometime in the evening you will spare a thought or two
For the beauty that emerges every spring.

The golden heads of daffodils that brighten every day the snowdrops are
Pure virgin white the crocus and forget me not that flutter in the wind.

Hurrying, scurrying, running around
Losing her purse and her keys.
Tripping, slipping falling about
Grazing her elbows and knees.

Caring sharing, giving her all
Unselfish as god would intend.
Long life, happiness that's what I wish
For Sheila my soft hearted friend.

Rene 1998

It's xmas 1983 and what a year it's been for me
I've served up tea and counted money
Mopped up floors which wasn't funny
Loaded parcels on a truck
Applied for jobs without much luck
Collected cash from fruit machines
And scrubbed out gentleman's latrines.

Now I'm busy selling wine
Moselblumchen from the Rhine
My pronunciation very poor
I struggle with le piat d'or
But as I cope with Christmas rushes
More and more I miss the buses
I'd give the world [my body too] ha ha
To be back there with all of you.

Snippets 6

Its ten to one I'm starving, where's my dinner
Its four hours since I ate and I'm no thinner
I'd rather stuff my face and be a sinner
Than live upon a diet of cottage cheese.
I guess I'd better get a drink of water
I'm like a lamb that's led unto the slaughter
I'm eating all the things I didn't orta.

He made the little spiders and although it's not too cute
He didn't want it flattened by someone's size ten boot.

The moths fly in the window and gather round the light
But if you pull their wings off they'll haunt you in the night.

Have you ever had a sausage in the pan
That spit and spluttered like a rude old man
And every time you tried to turn it round
It rolled right back so just one side got brown.

When you can see a patch of blue
In the sky large enough to make an
Elephant a waistcoat you can be
Sure it will be a nice day

Johnny palmer is like a patch of blue.

Gone the dreams I dreamed of you
Transporting me to pastures new
Silent now the haunting tune
Played on the far side of the moon.

Snippets 7

Don't walk away without a fond farewell
We may not have another chance to speak
The angels sleep is just a breath away
So place a loving kiss upon my cheek.

The wise old owl spoke up and said
By sharing out the pieces.
Were free to fight our greatest foe
The human being species.
Then in the north Atlantic
Before the midnight hour.
The penguins, polar bears
And seals came to power.

Concentrate while on the throne
On all the many things you own
The vacuum cleaner that you use
Could any minute, blow a fuse.

I opened my eyes and saw the sun
Another new day in my life had begun.
The trees were in blossom, the sky clear and blue
And over the hedgerows a butterfly flew.
A rainbow of colours were spread on the ground
As the perfume of flowers meandered around.
I saw sparkling eyes and a smile on each face
And I wished peace and love for the whole human race.

I opened my and saw the rain
At first I was tempted to close them again.
The trees stark and leafless, the sky dark and grey
No visible beauty in nature today.

Snippets 8

Ah cruel world that takes your strength and hides
It out of reach and leaves the body languishing in pain.
Through misty eyes you watch with longing as the flowers
Grow and wonder will you plant and reap again.

Such pleasant tasks so easy when the hands were strong
With youth neglected now as weakness calls the tune.
But in my heart I know you will regain your strength
Again to work on your beloved garden soon.

Missing you

I never thought that loneliness could fill a crowded room
Or tears could slowly drown you from a sentimental tune.

The joy of fleeting freedom could evaporate too soon
At the thought of never seeing you again.

Well I would rather dance with the devil on a cold dark night
Sell my soul to Satan if the price was right.

Desecrate the universe and blow it out of sight
But I'll never say goodbye to you again.

Life

Life can be tough when the going gets rough
And we all have to face up's and downs.
But the circus folk say when you have a bad day
That's the time you send in the clowns.

So, please pretty sue may I move in with you
For it won't cost a penny to feed me.
If you don't like my face, stand me in a dark place
But I'll always be there if you need me.

Snippets 9

IF CARS BECOME ELECTRIC
AND THE SKY TURNS EMERALD GREEN.
IF SPACESHIPS LAND ON DOORSTEPS
TO DELIVER MILK AND CREAM.
IF ELEPHANTS TURN SUMMERSAULTS
AND FISH LIVE UP A TREE.
NO MATTER HOW LIFE CHANGES
YOU CAN ALWAYS COUNT ON ME.

YOUR FRIEND
RENE MCDERMOTT

Lucky Me

I've felt the sorrow, shed the tears
And had my share of happy years.
Climbed a mountain, reached the heights
And fought my way through lonely nights.
Watched a flower fade and die
And heard a new born baby cry.
Sung the strain of loves sweet song
And felt the pain when things went wrong.
Known the worth of loving friends
And bitterness, when friendship ends.
I've looked with wonder at the sea
And shook with rage at destiny.
Experienced the joys of spring
And feared what would the winter bring.
Considered gold for what it's worth,
But chose the flowers from the earth.
Given hope to troubled friends
And when in need I've leaned on them.
What more could I want from life
I've coped with all the joy and strife.
So when my name you next recall
Say—lucky Rene—she had it all.